GOLDEN HART GUIDES
THE LAKE DISTRICT

GOLDEN HART GUIDES

The Lake District

John Parker

SIDGWICK & JACKSON LONDON
in association with Trusthouse Forte

Front cover photo: Ashness Bridge
Back cover photo: Rydal Mount
Frontispiece: Watendlath

Photographs by the British Tourist
Authority, with the exception of
ps 10/11, 13, 15, 16, 18 (Mansell
Collection)

Compiled and designed by Paul Watkins
Editorial associate: Jo Darke
Maps: John Flower

First published in Great Britain 1984
by Sidgwick & Jackson in association
with Trusthouse Forte

ISBN 0-283-99087-2

Photoset by Falcon Graphic Art Ltd,
Wallington, Surrey
Printed and bound in Great Britain
by Hazell Watson and Viney Limited,
Aylesbury, Bucks
for Sidgwick & Jackson Limited,
1 Tavistock Chambers, Bloomsbury Way,
London WC1A 2SG

Contents

Introduction

Over the last two centuries, libraries of books have been written about the Lake District. The literature has included a great deal of cloyingly sweet romanticism, and much repetition of the praise of previous writers. Many potential visitors could be deterred by the sheer weight of eulogy lavished upon the region's scenery; and it is probably too easy to get the impression that the Lake District National Park in the County of Cumbria is a series of pretty pictures to be admired at a distance, or at best a large ornamental water garden. But the Lake District to those who know it is an experience: clean, moving air to breathe; mountains rounded and easy to walk, or rough and craggy, and a challenge; clear water to boat on. And so much uncluttered living landscape always changing with the seasons, from light green through gold to bronze; and the patterns of light and shade. Peaks and valleys, lakes and tarns, rivers and waterfalls, open hill or wooded sanctuary: here is everything that is best in British scenery. It is impossible to describe the Lake District dispassionately and objectively. It demands a personal response.

In simple terms, Cumbria is the second largest county in England. The Lake District area, 880 square miles of which forms Britain's largest National Park, is a pattern of mountain ridges radiating from a high centre, containing within its many dales some 16 lakes, and with many mountain pools, rivers and streams. The streams are here called becks, the mountain pools tarns, and the mountain ridges, fells. There is generally no direct road communication across the central heights.

But that is too simple: within the broad framework lies the detail. Some of the valleys contain smaller valleys which themselves contain even smaller ones. The radiating pattern is broken by geological faults and glacial erosion channels. The structure is so complicated that it would take more than a lifetime to explore.

The varied rock formation has its effect on the landscape, changing it from north to south thus: first there are the Solway plains, then the bulky angular fells area, through the sharp jagged and craggy volcanic fells of the centre, to the rounded tree-clad fells of the southern Lake District, and through the limestone scars and plains to Morecambe Bay.

Each changing scene enhances the next; each variation attracts its devotees. There is the placid Wordsworth country around reed-rimmed Rydal Water; and Grasmere in its bright green fields.

Crummock Water

Some are affected, as John Ruskin was in childhood, by the dramatic view over Derwent Water into the tree-clad crags of the Jaws of Borrowdale from Friar's Crag, an easy level stroll from Keswick's boat landings. Photographers aim for the classic view from above Ashness Bridge on the Watendlath road from Borrowdale, with the arched bridge in the foreground, and Derwent Water and the mountains behind. Then not too far beyond, and an easy walk from the road, there is the scalp-tingling 'Surprise View' from Ashness Wood on the precipice overlooking Borrowdale and the lake. One could argue the merits of hundreds more accessible views from easy walks – across Windermere from Brockhole, the National Park Centre; across Ullswater from the east shore; across Coniston Water from Brantwood; or across Wast Water to the Screes. The fit fell walker will swear 'the higher the views, the better'. Boat enthusiasts will be satisfied with the ever changing scene across the gunwales to the tree-girt shores. The angler will choose his pitch, and savour it.

The Lake District of course is internationally famous for its literary associations: for the Lake Poets, with Wordsworth in particular (his ghost is everywhere); with de Quincey following Wordsworth to Grasmere; with Southey and Coleridge at Keswick. John Ruskin, writer, artist and social reformer, spent his last years at Coniston. Many 19th-century literary giants stayed here briefly, among them Sir Walter Scott, Tennyson, Keats, Dickens and Carlyle. Two popular children's writers were Arthur Ransome of Windermere and Coniston Water, and Beatrix Potter, whose little cottage at Sawrey is visited by thousands each year.

The tranquil surroundings hide much of the violent history of the disputed border country, which was once part of Scotland. No other castle in Britain has endured so many repeated attacks as Carlisle's, and the scenic ruins of the Norman castles at Brougham, Brough, Appleby and Penrith show the cycles of damage and repair. The same conflicts touched the abbeys, but the glowing red sandstone walls of Furness Abbey testify to the resilience of medieval religious power. Two other scenes, even more ancient, are outstanding. Castlerigg Stone Circle near Keswick stands in a natural amphitheatre ringed by mountains, and the view of the ruined Roman fort, perched on a plateau high above Eskdale by Hardknott Pass, is quite stunning. There is nothing quite like it anywhere else in Britain.

It is thought that the great sports of the county have historical

Windermere from Bowness

origins. At the colourful sports days and shows there are 'Cumberland and Westmorland' wrestling, and leg-breaking fell races, thought to have Viking origins. The other popular sport, hound trailing – where hounds race round a long course following the scent of an aniseed 'drag' – must date from the days when hounds were trained to lead herdsmen at speed on 'hot trod', in pursuit of border cattle-thieves on ground scent. The dales' shows give the full flavour of this unique region. They are the essential holidays for the fell farmers and their families. Hill farming is a main industry, and forestry another; neither seriously conflicts with the need for public recreation in an unspoilt countryside.

Details of the area's many attractions and activities will be found in 'The Best of the Region' section of the book, together with a selection of walks and motoring tours. The Gazetteer provides a round-up of the principal places of interest.

How Lakeland was Formed

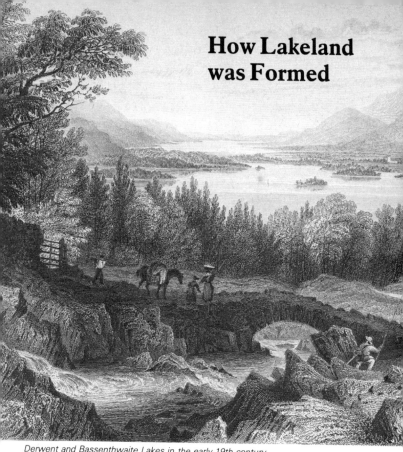

Derwent and Bassenthwaite Lakes in the early 19th century

The Rock Few other parts of the British Isles show so much geological diversity in so small an area. To understand and appreciate it one must stretch one's mind back into the immense depths of the earth's geological past, and imagine the present Lake District subjected to periods of volcanic activity, erosion and submarine sedimentation. Over millions of years, successive layers of rock were formed, each layer several miles thick.

The angular lines of the fells around Keswick and through the north-west, and isolated in the south-west around Black Combe, are formed from the friable *Skiddaw Slates* which were built up as a sediment of mud and grit deposited in the Ordovician sea 450 to 500 million years ago. These are the Lake District's oldest observable rocks. The crags of the central and eastern fells were formed from hard, varied materials we now call the *Borrowdale Volcanics*, which resulted from intense volcanic distur-

from Coniston past Tarn Hows and Windermere north-east to Kentmere. The mainly grey *Silurian Slates* and mudstones we see now around Windermere and to the south were formed of eroded silt, mud and grit, which built up rapidly on the sea bed during further storms and earth movements over the Silurian period, 400 million years ago.

The Skiddaw Slates, Borrowdale Volcanics and Silurian Slates form the main mass of the rocks visible in what we now call the Lake District. But later geological periods had a continuing impact on the character of the landscape.

From the start of the ensuing Devonian period (400-350 million years ago) we can imagine all the Lake District again engulfed by the sea. The different rock formations reacted characteristically to the severe earthquakes and upheavals that followed, the Silurian Slates fragmenting, the Skiddaw Slates crumbling and folding, the harder Borrowdale Volcanics fracturing and faulting. Intense friction heat in the Skiddaw Slates baked and altered the composition of some of the rocks. Great masses of boiling magma pushed through weaker inner crusts and formed 'blisters', then cooled slowly beneath the surface to produce the large-crystalline stone we call granite. One such 'blister' we can see exposed round Shap to the east, where the granite quarries prosper. Granite can also be seen in its various forms and colours in Eskdale, Wasdale and Ennerdale in the south-west.

Later, in the Carboniferous period (350-280 million years ago), submarine deposits rich in mollusc shells, crinoids and corals created a

bances, mainly in the central area, when lava flows and showers of ash and dust formed a coating at least two miles thick. Gentler earth movements at the end of the Ordovician period broke up the harder materials and forced through the softer, which were then eroded by storms to settle in the sea as mud and silt; molluscs active at this time added their shells to these deposits which we now call *Coniston Limestone*. Although barely visible, they form a distinctive, narrow band

11

canopy of limestone. This was shaken off outwards from the centre of the district when violent earth movements lifted the land high above the sea. Then, during a period of Sahara-like conditions, abrasive sand swept by hot winds tore away the surface of the land: sand drifts, some reddened with iron, filled the valleys around the limestone ring. This remains as New Red Sandstone, most notably seen in the buildings around Penrith and Furness, and in the castles and abbeys nearby.

The final shape of the Lake District was decided over the Tertiary period some 50 to 60 million years ago when enormous subterranean movements all over the earth thrust up the Alps and the Himalayas. The main impetus in this region came under the Scafells, and created a dome scarred with faultlines and eroded gullies. At this time the climate was mild and warm: storm waters drained off the dome in a radiating pattern, and gullied down the cracks and faults. The sea had receded and Britain was joined to the European continent. Thus it was until around a mere million years ago, when came the final catastrophe: ice.

The Ice The cause of the dramatic change in climate which heralded the Ice Ages is subject to speculation, but the effect can be seen. A glacier carries much rock debris of varying hardness at its base, and this material acts as an enormous grater. So the dome-shape of the Lake District was gouged out, filed and honed. In places where the glaciers penetrated, rested and then shrunk back, we can see the exact shape of their resting place in hanging valleys and tarns. The glaciers covering the high dome pushed outwards, meeting ice from the Scottish mountains, carving away the plains around the Solway Firth and scouring east through the Eden Valley. The lakes were formed as the valley floors were ground away, sometimes to below sea-level. Ice remained on the north and east of the mountain tops which the summer sun could not reach, and minor glaciers had their local effect. After the Ice Ages, and before the land became stabilized by plant cover, massive erosion was caused by storms.

The Result The story is, of course, over-simplified, but at least offers some definition of the landscape the traveller will discover: the clean-cut, angular shape of Skiddaw and the Skiddaw Slates to the north and north-west; the high, bulky crags of the Borrowdale Volcanics, from the Scafells and Great Gable through Borrowdale in the north and Coniston Old Man in the south, and east from Helvellyn to High Street; the tree-clad southern hills of the Silurian Slates around Windermere, spreading west to Coniston; the surrounding gentler landscapes of limestone and sandstones in the Eden Valley, and the Furness and Solway plains.

In the period following the Ice Ages, relatively little has changed; man has made his small mark through farming, grazing and deforestation, by afforestation and quarrying. To identify the local rock, one has only to look at the material in the nearest dry-stone wall, for the builders of the Lake District's old boundary walls took the stone nearest to hand.

The Lake District

A Brief History

Giant's Grave, Penrith

Prehistory The moving glaciers of the Ice Age 'wiped the slate clean' of any evidence of former human settlement in the Lake District. Flint artefacts found on the west coast suggest the presence of hunter-fishermen around 4500 BC, and archeological evidence points to an extensive settlement of people of the Neolithic culture from about 3500 BC. They cleared the forest, cultivated crops, and grazed cattle. Between 2800 BC and 2000 BC, they brought the area its first major industry. They had discovered a vein of very hard volcanic 'tuff', high on the central fells, which broke conchoidally, like flint when shaped by a hammer. We know now that there were several stone axe-factories working this rock. One such was by Pike o' Stickle in the Langdale Pikes, and there was a large one on Scafell Pike. Others may be discovered. The 'rough-outs' from the factory were polished and sharpened in the coastal sandstone areas. These were precision instruments, and were 'exported' – possibly from the port of Ravenglass – to other parts of Britain and even to Europe.

The most impressive man-made feature of the ensuing Bronze Age was the series of mysterious stone circles, many of which – most notably Castlerigg in Keswick and Long Meg and her Daughters – still survive. Following them were the stone wall enclosures and earthworks, thought to be of the Iron Age culture. One such walled settlement near Crosby Ravensworth was important enough to cause the Romans to divert a road to it. A large enclosure on Carrock Fell was probably a stronghold of the Brigante tribe.

13

The Romans It was the Brigante tribes of northern England whom the Romans found very troublesome after the conquest – though in theory these tribes had submitted to Roman rule by 47AD. In 79AD Gnaeus Julius Agricola came north to settle the matter permanently, building a series of forts to protect his roads: by 84AD he was in Scotland. The many wooden forts he built were replaced by stone ones under Trajan (98-117), and later by Hadrian (117-138). The remains can be seen, most strikingly on the fell-side high above Hardknott.

By 122AD, Hadrian had decided to build his great wall across England from the Solway through Carlisle to Whitby on the east coast. The object was not only to define Roman territory, but also to 'divide and rule' by splitting up the fractious tribes and thereby prevent the formation of dangerous alliances. By 138AD the wall had so consolidated the Romans' position that they were able to invade Scotland and build a new wall – the Antonine – between the Clyde and the Forth. This, however, was only a temporary line, the Romans having to retire to the old wall when the tribes later revolted.

Between 211 and 296 there was peace, and the villages – particularly Carlisle – grew and prospered around the Roman forts. In the following century, however, there was renewed unrest, and the wall changed hands several times. In 383 the Romans abandoned the wall, and by the early 5th c. they had left Britain for good.

Angles, Danes and Vikings The Romans left a fairly civilized Celtic community, but there were soon Anglo-Saxon incursions in other parts of Britain. After 615, the Celts were cut off by the new settlers and isolated in south-west England, south-west and northern Scotland, Wales and the north-west of England. The two last groups called themselves 'Cymry': hence Cumberland and Cumbria. The Cymry of the north-west were linked across the Roman Wall and the Solway with Scotland, as part of the Kingdom of Strathclyde.

The next wave of settlers came from the east. The Danes got no further than Carlisle and the Eden Valley, but the Vikings moved into Cumbria from their bases in Ireland and the Isle of Man, first as raiders, then as peaceful settlers. Towards the end of the 10th century, many came as Christian converts. The Viking Cross at Gosforth is a sign of this, and the close presence of an Anglian Cross at Irton suggests that the Vikings had no quarrel with their neighbours. They were not, after all, competing for the same land: the Angles wanted coastal plains where they could use their ox ploughs, while the Vikings preferred the hill-grazing of the interior for their sheep.

The abundance of Irish-Viking place names in the Lake District suggests extensive settlement. The word 'thwaite' means 'a clearing' (Haverthwaite, Braithwaite, Seathwaite); 'saeter' is 'shieling of summer pasture' (Seatoller, Satterthwaite, Ambleside – Hamal's shieling). Valleys are dales (*dalr*); the hills are fells (*fjall*); streams are becks (*bekkr*). Did the Vikings use the Celts as shepherds? The old way of counting sheep – 'yan, tyan, tethera, methera, pimp...' has echoes in the Welsh language.

Carlisle Castle in the 18th century

The Normans The Norman incursions did not at first affect Cumbria, which remained by agreement part of Strathclyde. But William Rufus on his accession did not accept this. In 1087 he took Carlisle and the north-west for England, settling the land with Saxon farmers. The new landlords built castles to hold their possessions, and religious houses were established to secure a foothold in the next world. However, landlords on both sides of the border disputed these arrangements, and up to 1214 the Lake District area was four times taken into Scotland and returned to England. The inhabitants of the moveable border could never be sure whether they were English or Scots: no doubt they could be whatever was expedient at the time. Such ambivalence – a pre-Roman tradition – would last for centuries.

In 1291 Edward I was asked to adjudicate in a dispute for the Scottish crown. Seizing this unique opportunity, he first demanded that all the claimants should accept him as the supreme ruler, and then chose John Balliol to take the crown. However, Balliol later betrayed the agreement when in 1296 he took his armies into England and burned some towns, including Carlisle. Edward's retribution was swift, earning him the title of 'Hammer of the Scots'. Balliol was defeated and captured, and governors appointed to rule Scotland for the king.

The Scottish people subsequently found a new champion in

15

William Wallace, who defeated the English at Stirling (1297) and carried out raids on Cumbria. Edward rushed northward again, but although he defeated Wallace at Falkirk (1298) he was unable to crush Scotland.

In 1306 Edward had to face another adversary. Robert the Bruce, Earl of Carrick, once a member of King Edward's court, fled to Scotland and there claimed the crown. After a series of clashes Edward mounted a campaign against Bruce, but on the march north died of natural causes at Burgh-by-Sands, within sight of Scotland. Bruce made several raids into England, and Edward II was no match for him. The English were decisively beaten at Bannockburn in 1314, and subsequently Bruce's troops pillaged and burned, without resistance, over the whole of Cumbria. Peace was finally concluded in 1328 and the Scots given their independence.

The Borderers Families living on the border were a continuing source of trouble. Blood feuds were common: not only Scot against English and *vice versa*, but Scot against Scot, English against English. The border had to be strongly policed on both sides by 'Wardens of the Marches', and Carlisle Castle played a leading part. Some notable wardens included Richard of Gloucester (later Richard III), John of Gaunt, and Warwick the Kingmaker. Cattle-raiding was one of the main occupations of the borderers, who could move swiftly on sure-footed ponies. Known as 'reivers' or 'moss-troopers', they wore home-

William and Mary Wordsworth

made armour, and carried long lances. Although border ballads later romanticized them, they could be vicious and cruel. They invented the term 'black-mail'; this was a 'black tax' which the farming communities had to pay for their protection.

The inhabitants of Cumbria had to learn to live with strife. The great lords had their castles, while the lesser nobles built their defensive pele towers, into which their families and retainers could flee, with their animals, at the approach of raiders. Communities also had their towers (church towers sometimes served this purpose) and one such can be seen at Newton Arlosh. The religious houses were particular victims of the raids.

When at last James VI of Scotland became James I of England, one of his aims was to end the border raiding. His method was summary and severe, with mass hangings at Dumfries in 1609. This harshly imposed peace lasted a long time, but there was to be one more violation in the rebellion of 1745, when the Jacobites marched across the border and Bonnie Prince Charlie proclaimed his father King from Carlisle Cross.

The mines Both the border raids, and the earlier Dissolution of the Monasteries, had had a damaging effect on Cumbria's economy. There were few alternatives, for the region's inhabitants, to bare subsistence farming. In 1564, however, the Company of Mines Royal began prospecting for various minerals around Keswick. Some fifty German mining experts were brought in, and they set up their colony of Derwent Island on Derwent Water. Major mines were opened up in the Newlands Valley and on Coniston Old Man. The mines produced copper, lead, silver and iron. The growth of mining and related industries had a considerable impact on the region. Keswick became a smoky industrial town. The becks provided water-power for the bellows of the smelting works, and the forests were devastated to provide charcoal. In the central Lake District the peak of prosperity was passed by the late 18th century, though new iron mines thrived in the west and south-west.

The 'Lakers' At this time a new industry was born, albeit with modest beginnings. The tourists had discovered the Lakes. Literature had stimulated their interest: Daniel Defoe, Thomas Gray, Celia Fiennes and William Gilpin had all visited the region. A very popular guide book appeared, written by a Furness priest, Father Thomas West. Captain J. Budworth wrote a stimulating account of his adventures in the Lakes, including fell ascents. And William Wordsworth was on the scene. He was born at Cockermouth and educated at Hawkshead, so he knew the area as well as anyone. In 1799, with his sister Dorothy, he came to live at Dove Cottage near Grasmere. There he worked on his *Guide to the Lakes*, which is still a best-seller. During his nine years at Dove Cottage he produced his greatest works, and other poets were attracted to the area.

Wordsworth's friendship and collaborations with Samuel Taylor Coleridge are well known. Coleridge lived for periods with another literary giant, his brother-in-law

Aira force, Ullswater in the early 19th century

Robert Southey, who moved into Greta Hall at Keswick. Thomas de Quincey took the tenancy of Dove Cottage when the Wordsworths left for larger premises, and his time there is described in *Confessions of an Opium Eater*.

Other writer-visitors of note were John Keats, Percy Bysshe Shelley (who lived at Keswick for a few months), and Sir Walter Scott, who included Cumbrian settings in *Redgauntlet*, *Guy Mannering* and the *Bridal of Triermain*. Harriet Martineau wrote a popular guide to the area, and she received George Eliot, Ralph Waldo Emerson and Charlotte Brontë at her Ambleside home. John Ruskin came to live at Coniston for the last 29 years of his life. At Mirehouse, by Bassenthwaite, the Spedding family were visited frequently by their friends Thomas Carlyle and Edward FitzGerald, and by Alfred Lord Tennyson, who wrote some Cumbrian atmosphere into his *Idylls of the King*.

Hardly a literary figure, but certainly a popular writer who brought even further interest to the Lake District, was Beatrix Potter who settled here and had a house at Sawrey. At her death she left much land to the National Trust.

The Conservationists. The National Trust was the brainchild of Canon Rawnsley and his friends. Rawnsley was the incumbent at Crosthwaite, Keswick in the late 19th century, and was unhappy at the way the land was being exploited by unfeeling people. He was echoing the fears that Wordsworth had expressed when he suggested that the Lake District should be 'a sort of National Prop-

erty, in which every man has a right and interest who has an eye to perceive and a heart to enjoy'. Rawnsley's idea was to acquire property by raising public subscriptions. The National Trust was formed in 1895, and it received much support from the growing number of tourists. The coming of the railway brought new prosperity to the region's manufacturing towns, but it was also a great boon to the tourist industry. Hotels and guest houses grew lavishly around Windermere and Keswick. More and more people had the opportunity to enjoy the countryside, and there was a need to conserve it and to make sure that the public could always have access to it. So the idea of 'National Parks' was mooted, particularly between the wars.

The National Parks and Access to the Countryside Act was passed in 1949. Ten National Parks were designated, the Lake District being the largest, with 880 square miles of land. Aided by the other conservation groups, the National Park Authority succeeded in preventing intrusive water extraction plans for Ullswater. It failed to get the improved A66 trunk road diverted from Bassenthwaite, even though the Government Inspector recommended this following the public enquiry. In the 1980s, plans to take water from Wast Water and to raise the level of Ennerdale Water were successfully opposed.

Fears are sometimes expressed that too many tourists can destroy what they come to enjoy. But the bulk of support for the conservationists comes from the tourists themselves, who have 'eyes to perceive, and hearts to enjoy'.

The Best of the Region

excluding City of Carlisle (p.52)

A summary of the places of interest in the region, open to the public. The location, with map reference, and description of each place, is shown in the Gazetteer. Names in bold are Gazetteer entries, and those with an *asterisk are considered to be of outstanding interest. (NT) indicates properties owned by the National Trust

Levens Hall

Churches

Those listed here are specially worth a visit, either for the building itself, or for some feature in or outside it.

Abbeytown Holm Cultram Abbey (St Mary's Church)

Appleby St Lawrence

Bassenthwaite St Bega

Beetham St Michael

† **Bewcastle** St Cuthbert

Bowness-on-Windermere St Martin

Brougham St Wilfred

Burgh-by-Sands St Michael

Carlisle see p.52

* **Cartmel** Priory Church

Crosby Ravensworth St Lawrence

Dacre St Andrew

Eskdale St Catherine

† **Gosforth** St Mary

Grasmere St Oswald

Great Salkeld St Cuthbert

Hawkshead St Michael

† **Irton** St Paul

* **Kendal** Holy Trinity

Keswick (Crosthwaite) St Kentigern

Kirkby Lonsdale St Mary

Kirkby Stephen St Stephen

* **Kirkoswald** St Oswald

Martindale St Martin

* **Newton Arlosh** St John

Patterdale St Patrick

Penrith St Andrew

St Bees St Mary & St Bega

St John's-in-the-Vale St John

Urswick St Mary & St Michael

Wasdale Head Church

Wreay St Mary

† See *Castles, Ruins, Monuments & Ancient Sites*

Historic Houses

Admission to most historic houses is
between £1-2.50 (children half-price).

* **Bassenthwaite** Mirehouse
Apr-Oct, Wed, Sun & Bank Hol Mon
2-5; Grounds daily

Belle Isle House
Mid May-Sep, Mon-Thur 10.30-5

Brantwood (Ruskin's home)
Easter-Oct, Sun-Fri 11-5.30

Cockermouth Wordsworth's House
(NT)
Apr-Oct, daily (not Thur) 11-5, Sun
2-5

Conishead Priory
Apr-Sep, Sat, Sun & Bank Hols, also
Wed & Thur in Aug 2-5

Dalemain
Easter-mid Oct, daily (not Fri) 2-5.15

* **Dove Cottage**
Apr-Sep, daily 9.30-5.30, Sun 11-
5.30; Mar & Oct, daily 10-4.30, Sun
11-4.30

* **Holker Hall**
Apr-Oct, daily (not Sun) 10.30-6

Hutton-in-the-Forest
Apr-Aug, Bank Hol Mons, also mid-
May to mid-Oct, Thur & last 3 Suns
in Aug 2-5

Keswick Old Windebrowe
Easter-Oct, Wed 2-4.30. Mon-Fri
9-4.30 by appointment

Levens Hall
Apr-Oct, Tue-Thur, Sun & Bank
Hol Mon 11-5

* **Muncaster Castle**
Apr-Oct, Tue-Thur & Sun 1.30-4.30;
Grounds daily (not Fri) 12-5

Rydal Rydal Mount
Mar-Oct, daily 10-5.30; Nov-Jan,
daily (not Wed) 10-12.30 & 2-4

Sawrey Hill Top (Beatrix Potter's
home) (NT)
Apr-Oct, daily (not Fri) 10-5.30, Sun
2-5.30 (or dusk)

* **Sizergh Castle** (NT)
Apr-Sep, Wed, Thur, Sun & Bank
Hol Mon, also Mon in Aug 2-5.30

Troutbeck Townend (NT)
Apr-Oct, Tue-Fri, Sun & Bank Hol
Mon 2-6 (or dusk)

Ulverston Swarthmoor Hall
Mar-Oct, Mon-Wed & Sat 10-12 &
2-5

Windermere (Lake) Rusland Hall
Apr-Sep, daily 11-6

Parks, Gardens & Wildlife
(See also *Nature Reserves*, p.29)

Admission to the gardens of historic
houses is usually included in a
combined ticket for house and
garden. (See admission to historic
houses above.) Where the garden
can be visited separately this is usually
about half the price of the combined
ticket. The entrance fee for other
gardens open to the public is usually
in the range 30-50p (children half-
price or less).

Ambleside Stagshaw (NT)
Apr-Jun, daily 10-6.30; Jul-Oct by
appointment

Appleby Castle Grounds
See *Castles, Ruins, Monuments &
Ancient Sites*

Bassenthwaite Mirehouse
House & garden. See *Historic Houses*

Belle Isle
House & garden. See *Historic Houses*

Brampton Talkin Tarn
Country Park. Open all year

Brantwood (Ruskin's home)
House & woodlands
See *Historic Houses*

* **Brockhole** Visitor Centre & Garden
See *Museums, Galleries & Visitor
Centres*

Carlisle Corby Castle Gardens
Apr-Sep, daily 2-5

Conishead Priory
House & garden. See *Historic Houses*

Dalemain
House & garden. See *Historic Houses*

Holker Hall
House & garden. See *Historic Houses*

Hutton-in-the-Forest
House & garden. See *Historic Houses*

Keswick Lingholm
Apr-Oct, Mon-Fri 10-5

Kirkoswald Nunnery Walks
All year, daily 9-8 (or dusk)

* **Levens Hall**
House & garden. See *Historic Houses*

Lowther Park
Lowther Wildlife Park
Apr-Oct, daily 10-5

* **Muncaster Castle**
House & garden. See *Historic Houses*

Rydal Rydal Mount
House & garden. See *Historic Houses*

Sizergh Castle (NT)
House & garden. See *Historic Houses*

Temple Sowerby Acorn Bank (NT)
Apr-Oct, daily 10-5.30

Windermere (Lake) Graythwaite Hall
Apr-Jun, daily 10-6

Windermere Holehird Gardens
Daily dawn-dusk

Castles, Ruins, Monuments & Ancient Sites

Unless otherwise stated, these sites are accessible at all reasonable times.

Ambleside Borrans Field
Roman fort foundations (NT)

Appleby Appleby Castle
Norman castle keep
Apr-Sep, daily 10.30-5

Barrow-in-Furness Piel Castle
Norman castle ruin

Bewcastle Bewcastle Cross
7th-c. cross in churchyard

* **Brough** Brough Castle
Norman castle ruin
Mar-Oct, Mon-Sat 9.30-6.30, Sun 2-6.30; Oct-Mar, Mon-Sat 9.30-4, Sun 2-4 (closed Dec 24-26, Jan 1 & 1st Mon in May)

* **Brougham** Brougham Castle
Norman castle ruin
Times as for Brough Castle

Burgh-by-Sands Edward I's Monument
Monument on Solway sands

Calder Abbey
Norman abbey ruin
Not open to public, but see Gazetteer

Carlisle see p.52

Carrock Fell
Romano-British defensive walls

* **Castlerigg Stone Circle** (NT)
Bronze Age stone circle

Crosby Ravensworth Ewe Close
Romano-British settlement

Dacre Dacre Castle
Norman castle
By written appointment only

Dalton-in-Furness Dalton Castle (NT)
14th-c. pele tower
Daily at reasonable hours (key at 18 Market Place)

Egremont Egremont Castle
Norman castle ruin

* **Furness Abbey**
Norman abbey ruin
Times as for Brough Castle

Gosforth
Viking cross in churchyard

Hadrian's Wall
Roman Wall remains

* **Hardknott Roman Fort**
Ruined walls of hillside Roman fort

Irton
9th-c. cross in churchyard

Kendal Kendal Castle
Norman castle ruin

Kendal Castle Howe
Early Norman castle earthworks

Kirkoswald
Norman castle ruin
Subject to landowner's permission

Lanercost Priory
Norman priory ruin
Times as for Brough Castle

* **Long Meg and Her Daughters**
Bronze Age stone circle

Mayburgh & King Arthur's Round Table
Earthworks of ancient stone circles

Penrith Penrith Castle
Norman castle ruin

Ravenglass Glannaventa Roman Fort
Ruin of fort's bath-house

Shap Shap Abbey
Ruined tower and foundations of Norman abbey
Mar-Oct, Mon-Sat 9.30-6, Sun 2-6; Oct-Mar, Mon-Sat 9.30-4, Sun 2-4

Shap Standing Stones
Bronze Age monument

* **Swinside Stone Circle**
Bronze Age stone circle
Close approach subject to landowner's permission

Ullswater Dunmallot
Hilltop earthworks of Romano-British hill fort

Urswick Urswick Stone Walls
Remains of Iron Age settlement

Museums, Galleries & Visitor Centres

Ambleside Doll's House Museum
Easter-Sep, Wed-Fri 10.30-1 & 2-5

* **Ambleside** Lake District History Centre
Mar-Oct, daily 9-6; winter by arrangement

Appleby Dyke Nook Working Farm Museum
Easter weekend & Spring Bank Holend Oct, daily 1-5

Barrow-in-Furness Furness Museum
Mon–Fri 10-5, Thur & Sat 10-1

Borrowdale National Park Information Centre (Seatoller)
Times as for Brockhole

Bowness-on-Windermere
Windermere Steamboat Museum
Apr-Oct, Mon-Sat 10-5, Sun 2-5

* **Brockhole** Windermere
National Park Visitor Centre
Easter-Oct, daily 10-5; Nov-Easter by arrangement

Broughton-in-Furness Hadwin Motorcycle Museum
Easter week & May-Sep, Mon-Sat 10-5, Sun 1-5

Carlisle see p.52

* **Coniston** Ruskin Museum
Apr-Oct, daily 9.30-8 (or dusk)

Dalemain Agricultural Museum
See *Historic Houses*

Dalemain Westmorland and Cumberland Yeomanry Museum
See *Historic Houses*

* **Dove Cottage** Grasmere & Wordsworth Museum
See *Historic Houses*

Grizedale Forest
Visitor & Wildlife Centre
Mar-Oct, daily 10-5; Nov-Easter by arrangement

* **Hawkshead** Grammar School
Daily (not Wed) 10-5

Holker Hall Lakeland Motor Museum
See *Historic Houses*

Kendal Abbot Hall Art Gallery
Jan 2-Dec 19, Mon-Fri 10.30-5.30, Sat & Sun 2-5

* **Kendal** Museum of Lakeland Life & Industry (Abbot Hall)
Jan 2-Dec 19, Mon-Fri 10.30-5, Sat & Sun 2-5

Kendal Museum of Natural History & Archaeology, Station Road
Jan 2-Dec 19, Mon-Fri 10.30-12.30 & 2-5, Sat 2-5

Keswick Fitz Park Museum & Art Gallery
Apr-Oct, Mon-Sat 10-12.30 & 2-5.30; groups at other times by arrangement

* **Keswick** Pencil Museum
Apr-Oct, Mon-Fri 9.30-4.30, Sat & Sun 2-5

Keswick Railway Museum
Mid Jul-early Sep, Mon-Sat 10-5, Sun 2-5; also Apr-Jul & Sep-Oct, Sat 10-5, Sun 2-5

Maryport Maritime Museum
Daily (not Wed & Sun) 10-12 & 2-6

Millom Folk Museum
Easter week, then Spring Bank Hol-Sep, Mon 11-4.30, Tue-Sat & Bank Hols 10-4.30

* **Penrith** Steam Museum
Apr-Oct, Mon-Fri 10-5, Sun 12-5

Ravenglass Railway Museum
Mar-Nov, daily 10-6; other times by arrangement

Ulverston Laurel & Hardy Museum
Apr-Oct, daily (not Wed & Sun) 10-4; other times by arrangement

Whinlatter Visitor Centre
Easter-Oct, daily 10-5

Whitehaven Museum
Daily (not Wed, Sun or Bank Hols) 10-5

Workington Helena Thompson Museum
Daily (not Sun & Mon) 2-4

Industrial & Rural Heritage

Alston South Tynedale Railway
Summer only

Barrow-in-Furness Furness Museum
See *Museums, Galleries & Visitor Centres*

Beetham Heron Corn Mill
Working flour mill
Daily (not Mon) 11-12.15 & 2-5

Cockermouth Wythop Mill
Restored sawmill
Summer only

Dalemain Agricultural Museum
See *Historic Houses*

Dove Cottage Grasmere & Wordsworth Museum
See *Historic Houses*

Eskdale Mill (Boot)
Working water mill
Easter-Sep, daily (not Sat) 11-5

Eskdale Ravenglass & Eskdale Railway
All year

* **Kendal** Museum of Lakeland Life & Industry
See *Museums, Galleries & Visitor Centres*

Kendal Goodacres Carpets Ltd,
Aynam Road
Carpet making
Wed & Fri tours at 2 & 3.30

* **Keswick** Pencil Museum
See *Museums, Galleries & Visitor Centres*

Millom Folk Museum
Mining Industry
See *Museums, Galleries & Visitor Centres*

* **Penrith** Steam Museum
Machine-shop, blacksmith, foundry
See *Museums, Galleries & Visitor Centres*

Penrith Weatheriggs Country Pottery, Clifton Dykes
Old kiln, steam-powered machinery, clay processing, weaving
Daily 10-5

Ravenglass Muncaster Mill
Restored water mill
Summer only

Salkeld, Little
Working flour mill (flour on sale, wholemeal café)
Easter-Oct, Wed, Thur & Sun 2.30-5.30; Sats in Jul, Fri, Sat & Bank Hol in Aug 2-5.30

Troutbeck Townend (NT)
Yeoman's house of the 17th c.
See *Historic Houses*

Windermere Lakeside & Haverthwaite Railway
May-Oct

Waterfalls

There are hundreds of waterfalls in the Lake District; below are a few of the accessible ones.

* **Ambleside** Stock Ghyll Force
Main fall 60ft, in a ravine

* **Borrowdale** Lodore Falls
Great volume; main fall 90ft

Colwith Falls (NT)

Easedale Sour Milk Gill
Rock Spill

Eskdale Stanley Gill Force
Main fall 60ft

Great Langdale Dungeon Ghyll
Force
60ft falls

Skelwith Force
15ft, but great volume

Taylor Gill Force
100ft, but approach for sure-footed
only

Tilberthwaite Gill
Viewpoint bridge; 60ft fall

* **Ullswater** Aira Force (NT)
Several falls in woodland valley

Viewpoints

There are thousands of viewpoints
in the Lake District. Below are a
few of the accessible views regarded
as 'classics'.

* **Ambleside** Jenkin Crag (NT)

Arnside Arnside Knott (NT)
Limestone peak

Castlerigg Stone Circle (NT)
Stones in foreground, Helvellyn
range beyond

Ennerdale Bowness Knott

Grange-over-Sands Morecambe
Bay
Flocks of wintering birds on the
sands

Keswick Castle Head (NT)
Panoramic view from a volcanic
'plug'

* **Keswick** Friar's Crag (NT)
Derwent Water and Borrowdale

Keswick Latrigg
View over Keswick and Derwent
Water

Kirkby Lonsdale River Lune
Views praised by Ruskin, painted
by Turner

Kirkoswald Nunnery Walks
River views

Little Langdale Blea Tarn (NT)

Loughrigg Terrace (NT)
View over Grasmere

Muncaster Castle
View from terrace

Penrith Penrith Beacon

St Bees Head
Sandstone cliffs

Scout Scar
View from limestone cliffs

* **Tarn Hows** (NT)
Famous beauty spot

Wast Water Wast Water Screes

* **Watendlath** Ashness Bridge (NT)
Most photographed view in Britain

* **Watendlath** Surprise View (NT)

Windermere (Lake) Adelaide Hill (NT)

* **Windermere** Orrest Head
One of the best, yet near the town

Famous Connections

Many famous – or simply unusual –
personalities have been connected
with the Lake District and Cumbria.
Details of their association will be
found in the Gazetteer entries

Barrow, Sir John Ulverston

Campbell, Donald Coniston Water

Carlyle, Thomas Bassenthwaite

Charles Edward Stuart Carlisle

Christian, Fletcher Cockermouth

Coleridge, Samuel Taylor
Grasmere, Keswick

Dalton, John Cockermouth

De Quincey, Thomas Dove Cottage,
Rydal

FitzGerald, Edward Bassenthwaite

Fox, George Ulverston

Haskett-Smith, W.P. Great Gable
(Nape's Needle)

Laurel, Stanley Ulverston

Nicholson, Norman Millom

Peel, John Caldbeck

Potter, Beatrix Sawrey, Troutbeck

Rawnsley, Canon Keswick

Romney, George Dalton

Ruskin, John Coniston, Kirkby
Lonsdale, Keswick

Scott, Sir Walter Dove Cottage, St John's-in-the-Vale

Southey, Robert Keswick, Lodore Falls

Tennyson, Alfred Lord Bassenthwaite

Turner, J.M.W. Kirkby Lonsdale

Walker, Rev ('Wonderful Walker') Dunnerdale

Walpole, Sir Hugh Borrowdale, Keswick

Wordsworth, William Cockermouth, Grasmere, Hawkshead, Dove Cottage, Rydal

Hotels & Historic Inns

† Non-residential inn
(THF) A Trusthouse Forte Hotel

Grasmere
The Swan (THF)
Grasmere LA22 9RF
Tel (09665) 551
A posting house used before the horses began the steady ascent up Dunmail Raise, *The Swan* was frequently visited by William Wordsworth, who wrote:

> Who does not know the famous Swan
> Object uncouth, and yet our boast,
> For it was painted by the host,
> His own conceit the figure planned,
> 'Twas coloured all by his own hand.

The host referred to was Anthony Wilson, a friend of the poet Coleridge. The inn was used by Sir Walter Scott in 1805.

Hawkshead
The Drunken Duck
Barngates, Hawkshead LA22 0NG
Tel (09666) 347
Once known as *The Barngate*, the inn is some 400 years old and changed its name in Victorian times. One day the landlady found six ducks, apparently dead, sprawled about on the ground before the front door. She picked them up, took them to her kitchen, and began to pluck them. Soon after she had finished they began to show signs of life. They had, in fact been drinking beer which had leaked from a barrel in the yard. She was horrified and

knitted little red jackets for them to wear until their feathers grew again. It is said that they recovered. From that day the inn has been known as *The Drunken Duck*.

Kendal
† *The Fleece*
Highgate LA9 4TA
Tel (0539) 20163
Established in 1654, the name of the inn indicates the importance of Kendal as the southern gateway to the Lake District when roads were poor and fleeces from the fell sheep were brought by packhorse. The inn is a three-storey building in black and white stucco. The upper storeys overhang and are supported by a row of pillars.

The Woolpack
Stricklandgate LA9 4ND
Tel (0539) 23852
Like *The Fleece*, *The Woolpack* is also 17th-c. and was one of the main centres for the Lakeland wool trade and a place where fell sheep farmers met the wool buyers. It also became an important coaching house and to serve this purpose was largely rebuilt *c.* 1781. The most striking feature is the enormous entrance to the old yard which occupies nearly half the width of the building. It was made to take the wide heavy waggons which replaced packhorses when the roads began to improve towards the end of the 18th c.

Keswick
The George
St John Street CA12 5AZ
Tel (0596) 72076
The oldest inn in Keswick, *The George* dates from Elizabethan times. At this period German miners dug ores of lead and silver in the local Goldscope workings. The miners paid their dues to the queen's officers at *The George*, the main centre of trade. It is said that unscrupulous traders also brought plumbago ore or 'wad', stolen from the mines of Borrowdale, to be sold at the inn.

In 1715, the Earl of Derwentwater, on his last visit to Keswick, called at the inn for a tankard of ale before riding away to join the rebellion which ended with his death on the Tower Hill scaffold. In the 19th c. it was a noted coaching inn used occasionally by Coleridge, Wordsworth and Southey. The late frontage is Georgian in style.

The Keswick Hotel (THF)
Station Road, Keswick CA12 4NQ
Tel (0596) 72020

Like the rest of Keswick, this well-known railway hotel is built of grey stone; its conservatory gave 19th-c. travellers direct access from the station. Surrounded by lawns, rockeries and flowerbeds, it overlooks the town beneath the slopes of Skiddaw.

The Royal Oak (THF)
Station Street CA12 5HH
Tel (0596) 72965

Also Elizabethan in origin, *The Royal Oak* was entirely rebuilt in the 18th c. and became the headquarters of the packhorse trade and, as the roads improved, a posting house and a halting place for stage coaches.

John Teather, the landlord at the beginning of the 19th c., moved to Carlisle and set up a coaching business on the route between Lancaster and Glasgow. In 1837 he was succeeded by his son but railway competition killed the trade and young Teather returned to Keswick where he, in turn, became landlord of *The Royal Oak*.

The hotel was frequented by Coleridge, De Quincey, Shelley, Southey and Wordsworth, and it was here that Sir Walter Scott wrote his *Bridal of Triermain* (1813). Stevenson and Tennyson also stayed at the inn.

Penrith
The Gloucester Arms
Great Dockray CA11 7DP
Tel (0768) 62150

According to tradition this was Dockray Hall, the residence (*c.* 1471) of Richard, Duke of Gloucester, who became Richard III. Over the entrance is a shield bearing his coat of arms with white boars as supporters.

In 1580 extensive alterations were made. The inn is built of stone, now faced with painted stucco. Inside are the original plaster ceilings with the ducal arms and some 15th-c. panelling.

† *The Robin Hood*
King Street CA11 7AY

A plaque on the inn states: 'William Wordsworth stayed here with Raisley Calvert 1794-5.' Raisley was the brother of William Calvert, an old school-fellow of Wordsworth at Hawkshead School. The poet was no doubt concerned for his sick friend who was consumptive. In fact, Wordsworth nursed Raisley for a time in William Calvert's farmhouse, near Keswick. Raisley died in January 1795 and left Wordswoth a legacy of £900.

Troutbeck
The Mortal Man
Troutbeck, Windermere LA23 1PL
Tel (09663) 3193

First built in 1689, the present building reveals little evidence of its history. The post sign, however, which stands by the roadside, shows two men, one happy and robust holding a foaming mug, the other thin and pale. This is a modern version of the original sign which was painted by Julius Caesar Ibbotson in the 18th c. to pay for his stay during a sketching trip. The original verse on the sign was:

Oh mortal man, that lives by bread,
What is it makes thy face so red?
Thou silly fop that looks so pale,
'Tis drinking Sally Birkett's ale.

Wasdale
The Wasdale Head Inn
Wasdale Head, Gosforth CA20 3EX
Tel (09406) 229

'The highest mountain, the deepest lake, the smallest church and the biggest liar' – this was Wasdale's boast when Will Ritson was landlord of *The Wasdale Head Inn*. Fellsman, Master of the Hunt and gifted raconteur, Ritson obtained his first licence in 1856 only, it is said, after repeated summonses for illegally selling alcohol; the liquor was brought from Whitehaven along an ancient mountain smuggling route.

This is the mountaineers' inn: it saw the golden age of rock climbing late in the 19th c., when customers included pioneer climbers like W.H. Haskett-Smith, who made the first ascent of Napes Needle in 1886.

Windermere (Bowness)
The Belsfield Hotel (THF)
Bowness-on-Windermere LA23 3EL
Tel (09662) 2448
Bowness grew as a 19th-c. lakeside
resort; *The Belsfield* is one of its most
splendid hotels. Built as the grand
Italianate residence of a local mine
owner (1830), it stands on a slope above
Bowness Bay and Belle Isle, looking
across at Claife Heights and at
Windermere's wooded west shore.

Burnside Hotel (THF)
Bowness-on-Windermere LA23 3EP
Tel (09662) 2211
This small, friendly hotel stands in
gardens and woods above the shores
of Windermere. Close to its peaceful
surroundings is Bowness Promenade,
busy as a calling point for steamers,
and with boats to be hired.

The Old England Hotel (THF)
Bowness-on-Windermere LA23 3DF
Tel (09662) 2444
The Old England stands in pleasant
woodland gardens overlooking Lake
Windermere. The original country
house of 1820 became a hotel in 1871;
since then it has established a
distinguished clientele. Notable visitors
include Kaiser Wilhelm II (1895), and
the Queen of Tonga, Salote Tupon
(1953). Among sporting people who
have visited the hotel are Miss M.B.
Carstairs, Lord Wakefield and Sir
Henry Segrave, who was the first man
to set a speed of over 100 mph on
water.

Windermere (Newby Bridge)
The Swan
Newby Bridge, Ulverston L12 8NB
Tel (0448) 31681
This is a large old coaching house
of three main storeys and a slate roof
with dormer windows. There is an
effigy sign of a white horse above
the main entrance. In 1855 Nathaniel
Hawthorne described his journey by
coach from Milnthorpe Station to
The Swan, 'which sits low and well
sheltered in the lap of the hills – an
old fashioned inn where the landlord
and his people have a simple and
friendly way of dealing with their
guests'.

The inn is close to the fine old
grey stone bridge of five arches which
crosses the River Leven as it leaves
Lake Windermere, and has 300 yards
of river frontage where there is fishing
for brown trout, sea trout and, after
July, salmon.

Festivals & Events

Many colourful events, from the well-
known horse fairs and agricultural
shows to ancient customs such as the
children's rush-bearing processions,
take place in Cumbria's towns and
villages. Some outstanding events are:

May *Cartmel* Races (Spring Bank
Hol)

June *Appleby* Horse Fair (2nd Tue &
Wed)

July *Ambleside* Rush-bearing
Procession (1st Sat) and Sports (Thur
before 1st Mon in Aug); *Carlisle*
Cumberland Show (penultimate Thur);
Holker Hall Lakeland Rose Show (2nd
week); *Penrith* Show; *Windermere* Lake
Festival (2nd week)

August *Ambleside* Sports (Thur before
1st Mon); *Carlisle* Great Fair (3rd Sat
for 10 days); *Cartmel* Races (Sat &
Wed after 1st Mon and Summer Bank
Hol) and Show (Wed after 1st Mon);
Cockermouth Show (Sat before 1st Sun);
Ennerdale Show (last Wed); *Gosforth*
Show (3rd Wed); *Grasmere* Rush-
bearing Procession (Sat nearest 5th)
and Sports (3rd Thur after 1st Mon);
Kendal Gathering: 17-day Festival;
Keswick Show (Summer Bank Hol
Mon); *Lowther Park* Horse Driving
Trials & Country Fair; *Patterdale*
Sheepdog Trials (Summer Bank Hol)

September *Brough* Hill Fair (30th);
Egremont Crab Fair (3rd Sat); *Eskdale*
Show (last Sat); *Grasmere* Lake Artists'
Society Exhibition (1st week);
Hawkshead Show (1st Tue); *Kendal*
Westmorland County Show;
Loweswater Show (3rd Thur); *Urswick*
Rush-bearing Procession (Sun nearest
29th)

October *Wasdale* Show (2nd Sat);
Wigton Horse Sales (last Wed);
Windermere Marathon (last Sun)

Sport & Recreation

Walking The Lake District is a walkers' paradise, whatever their capabilities. There are many hundreds of miles of public Rights of Way throughout the county, and hundreds of square miles of open access land. Anyone who can read a map can enjoy walking as long as plans are not too ambitious. A selection of walks in the area is given on p.30.

Fell walking is a different matter, and only experienced and fit walkers and map readers should venture on the heights. There are more mountain rescues in the Lake District than any other part of Britain – well over a hundred each year. The terrain is rough and broken, and navigating can be difficult at first to those who have only walked on open moorland. The prudent will observe a few safety rules: use a large-scale map and carry a compass; wear well-cleated footwear; carry, or wear, windproofs and waterproofs; carry spare clothing, a torch and plenty of food; leave word of the intended route with someone; do not make over-ambitious plans; remember that conditions above bear no resemblance to conditions in the valley; 'phone the Lake District Weather Forecast Service first: (09662) 5151. Winter fell walking is only for the well experienced walkers. Ice axes, and sometimes crampons, can be necessities. Advice can be had from the National Park Ranger Service.

Nature reserves Most of the Lake District's nature reserves are open by appointment only. The main ones are:

Hay Bridge Nature Reserve
See *Windermere (Lake)*
　Apply to: The Warden, Low Hay
　Bridge, Bouth-by-Ulverston. Tel
　(022986) 412
Ravenglass Gullery Nature Reserve
See *Ravenglass*
　Apply to: Country Land Agent,
　Arroyo Block, The Castle, Carlisle
St Bees Nature Reserve
　Public access
South Walney Nature Reserve
See *Barrow-in-Furness*
　Apply to: Cumbria Trust for Nature
　Conservation, see below

About 30 reserves are administered by the Cumbria Trust for Nature Conservation; most are open to members. For information, apply to the Trust's Administrative Officer at Rydal Road, Ambleside. Tel (09663) 2476

Nature Trails varying in length from a few hundred yards to 5m or more can be followed from viewpoints or beauty spots throughout the Lake District. The standard of upkeep is variable. Locations and Information Points at:

Appleby Castle (Details of opening
　times at Castle entrance)
Arnside Knott (NT Information
　Centres)
Bassenthwaite Dodd Wood (Car park)
Belle Isle (Details of opening times
　from shop at house)
Brantwood (Details of opening times
　from house)
Brockhole (at starting point)
Derwent Water Friar's Crag (NT & NP
　Information Centres)
Ennerdale Nine Becks or Smithy Beck
　(Bowness Point car park)
Grange-over-Sands Hampsfell (Tourist
　Information Centre)
Grizedale Forest Millwood Forest Trail
　including Silurian Way (Information
　Centre)
Kendal Serpentine Woods (at 31
　Serpentine Road)
Loughrigg Fell (NT & NP Information
　Centres)
Muncaster Castle (Details of opening
　times at starting point)
Nether Wasdale (NT & NP Information
　Centres)
Thirlmere Launchy Ghyll or Swirls
　Forest (at starting points)
Whinlatter Forest (Visitor Centre)
White Moss Common (NT & NP
　Information Centres)
Windermere Lake Claife Shore (NT &
　NP Information Centres)

Guided Walks Accompanied walks are also available at many of the Lake District's major centres. Inquire NP information offices.

Boating Windermere, Coniston Water, Derwent Water, and Ullswater are highways, and boating can take place as of right provided that launching is made from public launching places, or with landowner's consent. Speeds of over 10 mph are, however, now *only* permitted on Windermere, and some stretches there have restrictions. All powered craft using Windermere have to be registered before launching, and numbers displayed. Registrations can be made at Information Centres or beforehand from the National Park Authority, Busher Walk, Kendal. Boats can be hired on several of the lakes: see the Gazetteer entries for each. There are a number of training centres for sailing, sail-boarding or canoeing. Launching sites for small boats are located all along the Cumbrian coast: details from Tourist Information Centres or the Cumbrian Tourist Board (see p.35).

Cycling The Cumbria Cycle Way pursues the outer boundaries of the Lake District, taking minor roads along the Eden Valley and the W flank of the N Pennines, following Hadrian's Wall and the Cumbrian coast, skirting Black Combe, and following the indented coast of the Furness peninsula with its estuaries and extensive sandflats. Information on the route and on cycle hire is available from the Cumbria Tourist Board (see p.35).

Fishing There is plenty of sport to be had in fishing for brown and sea trout, salmon, char, perch and pike in the lakes and rivers, but a licence is necessary from the North-West Water Authority for anyone over 10 years old. Very often the fishing-tackle shops are licensing agents and they usually also sell permits which are needed for most waters. Tourist Information Centres can advise if necessary. The Water Authority's *Guide to Fishing in the North-West* is useful, and is sold in outdoor sports' shops, or it can be had from: The North West Water Authority, Rivers Division, PO Box 12, New Town House, Buttermarket Street, Warrington, Cheshire.

Riding There are a good number of riding and trekking establishments in Cumbria, and a full list can be obtained for a small charge from: The Cumbria Tourist Board (see p.35). Horses and ponies can be hired, and there are schools for all levels of tuition, some of them able to cater for the disabled. Riding, of course, is only permitted on bridleways which are shown on large-scale maps. However, the terrain is rough, and trekkers are usually escorted by the Centres' personnel. Anyone bringing animals is advised to consult with the Secretary of the Cumbria Bridleways Association, Chairman Mrs T.P. Fell, Whitegates, Backbarrow, via Ulverston.

Rock Climbing There are rock climbs of all standards, for this is where the sport began. As in fell walking, the basic safety rules for rock climbing should be followed. Newcomers intending to climb should first read up on the climbs in the guide books available at mountain equipment stores. At high season the crags in Langdale and Borrowdale can be busy, and it is wise to think of other areas.

Swimming Even in hot weather the water in the lakes and rivers can be very cold. Another danger is that the lake-edge beds are normally steeply shelved: a 3ft depth can suddenly become 20ft. Lone swimming is not a good idea. Distances are hard to judge, and cross-lake swimmers should be accompanied by a boat.

Walks

There is no need to be an athlete or a mountaineer to get full enjoyment out of walking in Cumbria. (See the notes on walking in *Sport and Recreation*.) There are lake-shore, riverside and valley walks in plenty. A few suggested circular routes are described here, and they should be undertaken with the help of a 1:50 000 or a 1:25 000 scale map. There are many other possibilities, and similar circular walks can be found described in *Lake District Walks for Motorists (Central, Northern and Western Areas)* and *Walk the Lakes*, both by John Parker (1983).

Walk 1 *Round Grasmere*

This is the Wordsworth walk, and can be combined with a visit to Dove Cottage, where the poet lived and worked. From Grasmere village church walk E, cross the A591 with care and go up the road opposite. Dove Cottage is a short way up here, with the museum behind. From here go up to a road junction by a farm, and bear right. Continue downward by White Moss Common (Rydal views) and cross the A591 again. Walk across the common to the river, go right and cross the footbridge. Go N along the river bank and to the lake shore. Follow the shore round by the W all the way until prevented by a fence. Follow the path up to the road and go right, down the road to the village/3m

Walk 2 *Round Rydal*

This route with Wordsworth associations can be combined with a visit to Rydal Mount, Wordsworth's home for the last 37 years of his life. Start at White Moss Common car park, by the A591 between Ambleside and Grasmere. From the E end of the upper car park on the N side of the A591 go N up the track. When a T-junction is reached with a better track, go right. Continue on this undulating track and path to Rydal Mount. Go down the hill from Rydal Mount. (Behind the church is Dora's Field, where Wordsworth planted daffodils for his daughter's delight – not to be missed in spring.) Cross the A591 with care and go right for a short distance, then left to cross the footbridge over the river. Go right to follow path by riverside wood and on to Rydal Water shore. Follow shore path. It leaves the shore and climbs. There is a stile on the right for the path back to White Moss, descending, but before taking it continue upwards for a short distance for a splendid view from Loughrigg Terrace over Grasmere/3½m

Walk 3 *Loughrigg Tarn and Skelwith Waterfalls*

Park at Elterwater village, or on the Elterwater Common car park. Walk SE alongside road (B5343) then in ½m turn left upwards on minor road. At T junction go left and in ¼m sharp right through gateway and onto a track going SE by Loughrigg Tarn. Follow the track through. (Look back over the tarn for a grand view of Langdale Pikes.) At track end go right to minor road, right for a few yards, then left down another minor road to Skelwith Bridge. Walk to bridge but do not cross it; go right by quarry showrooms and workshops to pick up the path by the riverside and past the waterfalls. Follow path beside Elter Water and by riverside to Elterwater village/4½m

Walk 4 *Round Buttermere*

This is a lovely walk by the lake shore most of the way. Park at Gatesgarth car park SE of Buttermere, or at the foot of Honister Pass. Walk along road NW and in a short distance go left on a track to the lake shore. Follow path along the shoreline round the promontory and on through the tunnel, and at the end of the lake incline right for Buttermere village. Turn left and go past *The Fish Hotel*, and at the path junction left again to the bridge at the end of the lake. Cross the bridge and go left by lake shore. At the end of the lake go left over bridge and on path towards farm and starting point/4m

Walk 5 *Latrigg Ascent from Keswick*

Start by *The Keswick Hotel*; go round to the N side and left by an estate to pick up a straight path going right, to cross the A66 by a bridge. Follow path round W side of Latrigg until a track is viewed coming up from the left. Turn sharp right and follow the zig-zags up the summit of Latrigg. (Glorious views over to Derwent Water.) Follow a path E through stile and left by a fence, then right to join a track. Go right to join a macadam road and go right along it. Either follow this road through or take the alternative parallel path in the wood below. Cross the bridge at A66. Go right at the junction to join road and back left to hotel/6m

Walk 6 *Derwent Water Shore*

From Keswick go down to boat landings, pick up a timetable for the boat service, and catch the anti-clockwise boat to Hawes End. On disembarking go S along lake-shore path. The path leaves the shore to avoid a bog but regains it shortly. At the

SW end of the lake the path leaves the shore to go round private property but regains it beyond to lake foot. Go left on causeway and across bridges (good views left) to road. Go left past *The Lodore Hotel* (divert right to see Lodore waterfalls) and left to jetty to pick up the boat back/3m on foot

Walk 7 *Ashness Bridge and Surprise View*
Start at the car park in Great Wood 1m S of Keswick on the Borrowdale road. Walk on to the bottom left (SE) of car park and pick up a path starting on left for Ashness. Follow this path which contours round the hillside. Join the minor road and go left to the little hump-backed Ashness Bridge. The best view of the bridge and its glorious background is from up the beck. Continue up the minor road through Ashness Wood and watch for the viewpoint close-by on the cliff edge (right). A surprise view indeed. Return down the road, pass the bridge and down to the Borrowdale road. Go right by lake-shore to Great Wood/3½m

Walk 8 *Esk Side and Stanley Gill Waterfall*
Either park at Dalegarth in Eskdale, or combine this walk with a ride on the narrow gauge steam railway from Ravenglass and disembark at the Dalegarth terminus. Walk NE towards Boot and at junction left for the village go right to pick up the track to the small St Catherine's Church by the river. Go left alongside the river bank to Doctor Bridge. Cross the bridge and go right to Low Birker and right again to riverside and on to a bridge in a wood. Cross the bridge and to left along the path and two bridges to a third bridge which has a view of the lower falls. Do not go beyond this. Option here to go back along the track to Dalegarth Hall NW; or the sure-footed with a head for heights should go back a little way then upwards on path left to join an upper path, and left again for a dramatic aerial view of Stanley Gill Force. Behind this a stile leads onto a field and a track can be picked up going right for Dalegarth Hall. Pass the Hall and over the bridge to road and to Dalegarth/5m

Walk 9 *The Mountain Road and Tarn Hows*
The walk starts at Hawkshead. Walk up behind the church and take the footpath going right to join a minor road. Cross it and take the path across the field signposted 'Tarn Hows'. This brings you to a road. Turn left up it. Go right at the first junction then right again by stile to Sand Ground. Join minor road at Sand Ground and go left. Right at T-junction and then afterwards go left on track. This goes between walls and rises over a brow. When it falls down the far side, go left over a stile for Tarn Hows. Turn left at the tarn side and go by any of the paths round the tarn. Watch for a viewpoint crowned with a stone on the right as you move to the S end. Join the minor road; follow this road S towards Hawkshead, but by the path running parallel in the wood right. This brings you to a crossroads; go right ahead towards Hawkshead, picking up the path across the fields on which you started/5½m

Walk 10 *Windermere West Shore and The Heald*
There are wet sections on this walk after rain. Start the walk at Bowness pier and go S and onto shore at Cockshott Point. Follow the path round to the ferry road and go right and cross the lake by ferry. Go right along the lake-shore road and track for 2m through Heald Wood to Belle Grange. Climb left up rough track through wood, and near the hill brow go left to continue S on high-level path (views over lake). Follow this through until it descends and joins a path and track which gradually improves. At T-junction go left and continue downward through wood on a rough path. Before reaching the lakeside road look for a short cut to right by Harrow Slack/6½m

Walk 11 *Ullswater Shore Walk*
Start at Glenridding and take the steamer service to Howtown. Go right from the pier on a path which leaves from the lake shore presently, and go round Hallin Fell by lake-side. The path leaves the lake at Sandwick. Go up the minor road left for a short

Dove Cottage

distance, then go right upwards beside wall and continue, bearing right towards lake. The path goes by the shore again; keep with it until it leaves to go S to a farm. At the farm go right on track, over the bridge to Patterdale. Go right for Glenridding, picking up the path on the left up the bank after the pavement runs out/6½m

Walk 12 *Arnside Knott and Cliffs*
Start at Arnside. Walk up through the village and at Y-junction go right (W), and keep bearing left to pick up a track and path climbing to Arnside Knott viewpoint. Leave viewpoint and go SW. Paths converge: go left and follow track to road. Go down the track almost opposite and past the ruined pele tower. Bear right to walk SW, avoiding caravan site road turnings. On reaching a gate go left of it by fence, go through a wicket gate and on towards the road right. Cross the road with care and go down the road opposite. Ignore caravan site turnings and go left on track to join the cliff path. Go on by White Creek and round the shore to path and promenade: but if the tide does not allow this go right NE by New Barns to village/8m

Motoring Tours

Each of these motoring tours is circular and can be started at any point. Names in brackets indicate places of interest. Allow the best part of a day for each tour.

Tour 1 *Six Lakes tour from Keswick*
Keswick – W on A66 for 1m, then SE through Portinscale – S by minor roads with views over Derwent Water – Grange, cross bridge, right up Borrowdale – ½m car park left (Bowder Stone) – continue up Borrowdale – Seatoller – W over Honister Pass and by Buttermere lake – onwards past Crummock Water – turn acute left for Loweswater – past lake, SW by minor roads for Lamplugh and Croasdale – SE on minor road to Ennerdale Water (car park, walks) – return to Lamplugh, join A5086 for Cockermouth – pass Mockerkin Tarn – Cockermouth (Wordsworth's birthplace, house) – A66 E for 5m, turn left at foot of Bassenthwaite Lake – over bridge and E for Castle Inn – S by A591 on E side of Bassenthwaite (after 4m car park left in wood, walks, book at refreshment room for Mirehouse visit and shore walk) – return to Keswick across A66 roundabout.

Tour 2 *Eden Valley and John Peel Country (minor roads)*
Penrith – A686 (Alston road) to Langwathby, cross bridge – to Little Salkeld (working corn mill) – NE along Glassonby road (on left, Long Meg and Her Daughters) – Kirkoswald – NW for Staffield (Nunnery waterfalls and walks) – NW Armathwaite – NW to Cumwhinton – over M6, SW for Dalston (optional diversion to Carlisle, leaving by A595 then left after 4m for Dalston) – SW for Caldbeck village (John Peel's grave) – E and S by minor road past Mungrisdale to A66 – left to Penrith.

Tour 3 *Coniston, SW Fells and Dales, Wast Water*
Windermere to Bowness, cross ferry – Far and Near Sawrey (Beatrix Potter's house) – by Esthwaite Water to Hawkshead (Wordsworth's school) – N and W for Coniston, divert right for Tarn Hows (beauty spot) – continue

to Coniston village – S down A593 for
Torver – S (as for Ulverston) by A5084
along lake shore – Lowick – W to
Broughton-in-Furness – W on A595
for 1m, turn right just before Duddon
bridge for Ulpha – NW over moor for
Eskdale Green – bear right on minor
roads to Wasdale – along Wast Water
shore (viewpoints) – left for Gosforth
(Viking cross in churchyard) – S on
A595 for Ravenglass (narrow gauge
steam railway and museum) – continue
by Muncaster Castle (gardens and
house) – S via Bootle for Silecroft
(optional diversion to good beach) –
NE to Broughton-in-Furness – E past
Lowick to A590 – turn left for Newby
Bridge – N by E shore of Windermere
to Bowness and Windermere

Tour 4 *Six Lakes Tour from
Windermere*
Windermere – A592 for Penrith at
mini-roundabout – Kirkstone Pass
(views) – by Brothers' Water –
Patterdale – Glenridding (access to pier
for boating) – Lake-side road for 2½m,
Aira Green (car park and access to Aira
Force Waterfall, left) – on by lake shore
to Pooley Bridge (optional diversion
up A592 for Dalemain, house and
museum) – B5320 to Eamont Bridge
– right down A6 for short distance,
then left on minor road to Brougham
(Norman castle ruin) – W on A66
(optional diversion to Penrith 1m) –
Threlkeld (after 1m optional diversion
left, Castlerigg Stone Circle) – Keswick
(view over Derwent Water past boat
landings at Friars' Crag) – A591
towards Windermere – after 5m turn
right for W side of Thirlmere (narrow
road) – join A591 again S to Grasmere
(Dove Cottage, Wordsworth's house
and museum) – by Grasmere Water
and Rydal Water to Ambleside –
Windermere

Tour 5 *Furness from Kendal*
Kendal – S on A6 – Milnthorpe –
Beetham village (water mill) – S to
Carnforth ('Steam Town' railway
trains, museum) – NW to Silverdale
– Arnside – Milnthorpe – N on A6 to
Levens Bridge (Levens Hall, house
and gardens) – left on A590 and to
Grange-over-Sands – S to Allithwaite

– Cark – divert right to Cartmel (village
and Priory church) – back to Cark –
right by Holker (Holker Hall, house
and grounds) – N along B5278 –
Haverthwaite – left to Ulverston (Stan
Laurel's birthplace, museum; also on
return journey) – A590 Dalton –
Barrow road for 1½m, divert left for
Furness Abbey (ruins, Visitor Centre)
– return to A590 to Barrow – E and S
to coast road via Rampside – along
coast road to Bardsea (after ½m
Conishead Priory, grounds and house)
– Ulverston – A590 to Newby Bridge
– N for Bowness-on-Windermere – E
via Crook on B5284 to Kendal

Grange-in-Borrowdale

Tour 6 *Old Westmorland from Kendal*
Kendal – S on A6 and A591 to M6
junction, cross to A65 – Kirkby
Lonsdale (village and church) – A65
E cross river and then left N on A683
– Sedbergh – A683 Kirkby Stephen –
N on A685 to Brough (ruin of Norman
castle) – W on A66 to Appleby (old
county town, churches, castle) – S on
B6290 to Orton – W and N to A6 and
Shap – N end of village, left for Rosgill
(Shap Abbey diversion) – SW and by
minor roads to Haweswater – return
N to Bampton – Askham – E by
Lowther (wildlife park) to A6 (Penrith
diversion left) – Shap – Kendal

Further Information The Cumbria
Tourist Board and National Park
Authority put out detailed leaflets on
leisure activities in the Lake District,
covering a wide range of subjects
including sports and recreation,
steamer and bus services, and
accommodation. Leaflets, maps etc.
may be obtained from the Cumbria
Tourist Board, Ashleigh,
Windermere, Cumbria LA23 2AQ
or The National Park Information
Office, Bank House, High Street,
Windermere LA23 1AF

Gazetteer

**This includes information
on the location, history and
main features of the places
of interest in the region.
Visiting hours for all places
open to the public are shown
in 'The Best of the Region'.
Asterisks indicate references
to other Gazetteer entries.
(NT) indicates properties
owned by the National Trust;
(NP) National Park**

Carving in Carlisle Cathedral

36

Abbeytown
B1

Village on B5302, 5m E of Silloth

The village is named from **Holm Cultram Abbey** which sat here in the vulnerable disputed land of the Border Wars. When the Cistercian order founded the abbey in 1150 it was in Scottish territory, the land gifted by Henry, son of David, King of Scotland. It held extensive properties and it prospered from an export trade of salt and wool from the nearby port of Skinburness. When Edward I, 'Hammer of the Scots' pushed the border back, he used the abbey as a base, which was remembered vengefully after Bannockburn. Robert the Bruce sacked it even though his father, the Earl of Carrick, was buried here. Much later the Dissolution (1538) almost completed the destruction caused by intermittent border hostilities, but the nave was preserved as a parish church (*St Mary*). Seen now, the structure is largely 12th-c., with a fine example of a Norman doorway and its impressive 16th-c. porch.

Allonby
A1

Village on W coast on B5300, 6m NE of Maryport

Once a fishing village, Allonby became a Victorian resort. Not realising expectations it survives as a modest retreat with the best beach in the area, and good views across the Solway into Scotland. The old *Sea Water Baths* with their Ionic columns (1835) recall the town's early development as a resort.

Alston
D1

Small town on A686, 21m NE of Penrith. EC Tue. Inf (in season): Tel (0498) 81696

Situated at a height of 921ft on the side of Cross Fell, some reckon Alston to be the highest market town in England. Stone houses roofed with heavy slabs of millstone grit, cobbled streets, the sloping market place, the alleyways and yards typical of border towns, old-style shop fronts and friendly traders give it great character. Lead was mined hereabouts in Roman times; the foundations of the protecting Roman fort are to the NW of the town. But it was in the early 19th c. that Alston became a boom town. Lead, silver, copper, iron and zinc were mined. The mine owners were Quakers who pioneered workers' welfare schemes. The 18th-c. *Quaker Meeting House* is in the main street, which rises steeply from *St Augustine's Church* (1870) with its steeple, and the Victorian-Gothic *Town Hall*. Cheaper foreign imports of metal resulted in a decline in late Victorian times.

The *Pennine Way* passes through Alston and there are some good walks centred on the town. The summit of *Cross Fell* (2930ft, the highest point in the Pennines) is to the S, and *Hartside Height* on the Penrith road gives sweeping views across the Eden Valley to the Lake District and Scotland beyond. This steep, winding road can be dangerous in wintery conditions.

The **South Tynedale Railway**, operated by a railway preservation society, runs 1½m N of Alston through the S Tyne Valley (summer only).

Ambleside
C3(A)

Small town on A591 at N end of Windermere lake. Event: Rush-bearing procession (1st Sat in Jul), Ambleside Sports (Thur before 1st Mon in Aug). EC Thur MD Wed. Inf (in season): Tel (09663) 3084. Nat Park Inf Centre: Tel (09663) 2729

Ambleside is one of the three busiest holiday resorts in the Lake District. It was once a town of many mills powered by the rivers feeding into Windermere, but it was already becoming popular to tourists in Wordsworth's day. He mourned the demolition of the distinctive houses of the old town to make way for 'modern' buildings 'which look as if fresh brought upon wheels from the foundry where they had been cast.'

The town's increased popularity in Victorian times completed the change. *St Mary's Church* (1854), with its prominent steeple, was designed by Sir George Gilbert Scott. Windows in the *Wordsworth Chapel* commemorate the poet and his family, and reflect the town's popularity with literary figures of those times. A mural painted by Gordon Ransom in 1944 depicts the annual rush-bearing ceremony, an ancient tradition renewed by the Victorians.

Little predating the era of the Lake Poets and the Victorian excursionists now survives, although accounts of history and tradition are to be found in the *Armitt Library*, a notable collection of books left by Miss Mary Louisa Armitt, housed in the local library (which also contains the *Ambleside Ruskin Library*). The oldest building, much painted and photographed, is the most bizarre. It is the tiny *Bridge House* (NT) spanning the River Rothay. Its origin is a puzzle. It might be the old summerhouse of the manor of Ambleside long since gone. It has been tea room, shop and cobbler's. In the mid-19th c. it was a home for the Rigg family, which included six children, and today it serves as an Information Centre for the National Trust. Nearby, in Fairview Road, is the **Doll's House Museum**.

½m S of the church is **Borrans Field** (NT) by the lake head. This is the site of Galava, a Roman fort. Only the foundations remain. It almost certainly commanded an undiscovered route from the fort at Kendal, over the western passes by Hardknott Fort to Ravenglass on the coast. Excavations have shown that there were two forts. The first dates from Agricola's advances around 79AD. It was replaced by a larger fort around 100AD. There is evidence to show that before this fort was abandoned in 400AD it was burned down several times.

With its many guest houses and hotels, Ambleside's popularity is based on its ready access to the district's great attractions. Windermere itself with the steamer pier and boat hire jetties at Waterhead, S of the town, is one, but there are easy routes into Langdale, Grasmere and Coniston. Excellent walks are all around. There are the much loved classics by *Rydal Water*, or by viewpoints on *Loughrigg Fell*, or on the slopes above the lake's E end by *Skelghyll Wood* and **Jenkin Crag** on Wansfell (NT). Fell walkers also find it a good centre, with *Fairfield* (2863ft) being the nearest challenge. One of the local attractions missed by many is the spectacular waterfall, **Stock Ghyll Force**, in a wooded ravine behind *The Royal Yachtsman Hotel*.

The town has its main museum, the **Lake District History Centre**, on Lake Road. Ambleside Sports, in August, include fell-racing and Cumberland and Westmorland wrestling.

On the A591 S of the town opposite the Waterhead Marina is **Stagshaw** (NT) a woodland garden with views over Windermere.

Appleby   D2

Small town on A66, 14m SE of Penrith. Event: Horse Fair (1st Wed in Jun). EC Thur MD Sat. Inf (in season): Tel (0930) 51177

Some Cumbrians still mourn the passing of the old county of Westmorland (swallowed by the new county of Cumbria in 1974), especially those in Appleby, for this was the County Town. The town has a distinctive character, an assertiveness born of historical strife; for it stands by the side of an ancient cross-Pennine route in disputed border territory. In fact it was a part of Scotland until William Rufus asserted Norman authority in 1092. It surrendered to a Scot of Norman descent, William the Lion, in 1174; was taken by Henry II and rebuilt as a royal burgh in 1179; retaken and burned again in 1314; and yet again laid waste in 1388 when it remained ruinous until the 16th c.

The **Castle** stands at the head of Boroughgate. It was originally built by Ranulf de Meschines in the late 11th c. It became a castle of the Clifford family, and Lady Anne Clifford restored it in the early 17th c. Shortly afterwards, the E side was majestically rebuilt in contemporary style, regretfully with stone taken from Brougham and Brough Castles. The Norman keep, '*Caesar's Tower*', survived with part of the 12th-c. curtain wall. It is open to the public, and the grounds contain a collection of rare breeds of farm animals. A short *Nature Trail* starts near the castle entrance.

At the top of the street, below the castle, is the 17th-c. *High Cross*, and down the street on the right there is an archway with a bell. Beyond is a cobbled courtyard and the *St Anne's Hospital Almshouses*, endowed for 'a mother, a reader, and twelve sisters for ever' by Lady Anne Clifford in 1653. Near the end of the street, with its fine Georgian and Victorian buildings, the 16th-c. *Moot Hall* divides the Street near *Low Cross*.

St Lawrence's Church was burned down twice by the Scots, and the tower, built sturdily as a refuge from raids in the 12th c., is the oldest part left. There is evidence of church restorations in three periods before the 18th c. The precious organ is partly 16th-c., and came as a gift from Carlisle Cathedral in 1684. A well preserved alabaster figure with a metal crown covers the tomb of Margaret, widow of George Clifford, Queen Elizabeth I's Champion. Nearby is Lady Anne's Monument, showing the Clifford family tree.

The 'Old Town', of which nothing remains, grew up over the bridge on the Eden's E bank. *St Michael's Church*, in Bongate, also suffered from the raids. The N wall is 12th-c., but there is much 19th-c. restoration. The church probably stands on a Saxon foundation. The N doorway has a Saxon 'hog-back' gravestone as a lintel.

Appleby's normal peace is shattered in June by the annual horse fair, an event going back more than 300 years. The caravans of gypsies and travelling folk arrive days before. On the day preceding the sale, the several hundred horses are shown off and races are organised. The unique event attracts large colourful crowds with attendant bustle and noise. At this time critics liken Appleby to a Wild Western town.

There are many pleasant walks around this friendly town, and it is a good centre for exploring the delights of the *Eden Valley*.

4m SE of Appleby on the A66 at Sandford is the **Dyke Nook Working Farm Museum** with a display of old farm and domestic implements.

Arnside
C4

Village on B5282, 3m SW of Milnthorpe. EC Thur

Sitting on the S side of the Kent estuary, Arnside was once a fishing village. It is now a modest holiday resort, though hardly 'sea-side' except at full tide. The sands are a haven for sea birds and waders; not so for bathers owing to mud content, and the tide rushes in at a dangerous speed. Hereabouts are lovely woodlands on limestone, with some excellent botanical walks, and a *Nature Trail*. Nearby **Arnside Knott** (NT) gives sublime views. Beyond the knott is the picturesque ruin of *Arnside Tower*, a 15th-c. pele tower. (See also *Walk 12, p.33*).

Ashness Bridge see *Borrowdale*

Barrow-in-Furness
B4

Pop 64,000. On Furness peninsula 8½m SW of Ulverston (A590/A5087). EC Thur MD Wed, Fri & Sat. Inf: Tel (0229) 25795

Barrow is a manufacturing and market town, with its shipyards the main industry. The town is very much a product of the Industrial Revolution, and most of its buildings date from the late 19th c. when it was laid out by a young industrialist, James Ramsden. His Barrow Shipbuilding Company of 1869 grew to become Vickers plc. Although the town offers nothing picturesque, there are two grand Victorian churches (*St George's and St James's*). The Town Hall, in Gothic style, is suitably imposing, and the approach by Abbey Road is very fine.

The **Furness Museum** in Ramsden Square contains a local bird collection, model ships, stone axes and other agricultural implements. *Walney Island*, 1½m W, is reached by a bridge. It has an excellent beach, and a bird sanctuary at the S end. On the tidal flat here is **Piel Castle**, the ruins of a Norman motte and bailey used as a refuge and store-house for the monks of Furness Abbey. There is access by boat from Roa Island to the N.

On the NE outskirts of the town is **Furness Abbey*, the ruin still isolated in its tree-clad valley.

Bassenthwaite (NP)
B2

Lake & settlements between A66/A591, 2m N of Keswick

Bassenthwaite is the northernmost of the sixteen lakes, receiving the outflow from Derwent Water of which it was once a part but from which it is now separated by an alluvial plain. It is about 4m long and ½m wide, and it is comparatively shallow, reaching just 51ft; it has silted more rapidly as its feeders pass through the softer shales of the Skiddaw Slates. Even though it is cursed by the close proximity of the A66 on the W, built here in spite of vigorous opposition from the National Park and the conservation groups, it is still a beautiful lake, walled by the great fells of Skiddaw to the E, with Lord's Seat and Barf to the W. The lake is in the ownership of the National Park whose policy is to retain the present level of activity. Power boats are banned.

The most atmospheric point of view is from the ancient **Church of St Bega** on the E shore, which is approached by lanes and paths from the A591. Away from any disturbing traffic the quiet little church offers the perfect foreground to the lake view. The church was built here in ancient times when the lake was the main highway, the roads being rough and boggy. The round churchyard suggests that this was a pagan site taken over by Celtic Christians. The rare dedication is to St Bega, a female Celtic saint. The church shows Norman structure in the chancel arches and doorways. The mounting block outside was almost certainly the base of an ancient cross.

To the SE of the church is **Mirehouse**, a manor house of 1660 with 18th and 19th-c. additions. This has been the house of the Spedding family since 1802, and has considerable literary connections. James Spedding was the personal friend of Thomas Carlyle, Alfred Lord Tennyson and Edward FitzGerald, all frequent visitors. Tennyson was a visitor in 1835 and the lake shore here inspired his vivid description of the King's departure in the *Morte d'Arthur*.

Mirehouse is open to the public (in the summer), and there are paths through the grounds down to the church and shore. A stone marks the spot where Tennyson would sit, and where he 'heard the ripple washing in the reeds, And the wild water lapping on the crag'.

Across the A591 from Mirehouse is a refreshment room in the estate's former sawmill. From the car park there are walks and a nature trail on the slopes of *Dodd Wood*, which overlooks the lake on a spur of Skiddaw.

There is limited access to the W shore. There is a car park at *Powter How Wood* (NP) by *The Swan Hotel*, which now sits peacefully by the old W road at Thornthwaite. From the wood there is an underpass below the A66 which gives access to shore land. Towering above the hotel is *Barf*; from its steep fell-side, and high above, is a rock said to suggest the shape of a bishop. *'The Bishop'* is whitewashed each year by a volunteer who is rewarded with a pint of ale.

There is lake shore access from lay-bys (NP) by the lake outlet at Ouse Bridge.

Beetham C4
Village off A6, 1m S of Milnthorpe

Beetham, just missed by the A6, has fine 17th, 18th and 19th-c. buildings. **The Church of St Michael and All Angels** sits four-square partly on Saxon foundations by the River Bela. It has distinctive Norman features: the tower is 12th c., and in the nave the S arcade is of the same period. The N arcade is 15th-c. Cromwellian troops are said to have used the church as a stable and inevitably are blamed for the damage to the two 15th-c. effigies, said to be of Sir Thomas Beetham and his lady. On the same bank of the river on a site occupied by a mill for over 700 years, sits the **Heron Corn Mill**. It has been restored as a working mill and is open to the public from April to September. It is approached by a track from the village, or from a visitors' car park by the paper mill.

Belle Isle C3(A)
Island on Lake Windermere offshore from Bowness-on-Windermere

Windermere is almost divided into two lakes in its middle reaches by this large island. On it is a very unusually designed *Round House*, built in 1774 for a Mr English, but later acquired by the Curwen family. J.C. Curwen was responsible for much of the tree planting which now beautifies the island and the E slopes of *Claife Heights* above the lake's W shore. The house, also called *Belle Isle*, is open during the week in the summer. An island *Nature Trail* starts nearby.

Roman occupation of the island was shown by traces of a Roman building found when the house was being built. Manor houses later occupied the site. One was occupied by the Philipsons, Royalists during the Civil War. The Roundheads, who lacked large guns, besieged the island unsuccessfully for 80 days. The siege was raised by Colonel Huddleston Philipson, fresh from a Royalist victory at Carlisle. The Colonel was nick-named 'Robin the Devil', probably because he is said to have ridden his horse into Kendal's Holy Trinity Church in search of one of his Cromwellian enemies, Colonel Briggs.

Bewcastle C1
Village (B6264 & minor roads), 25m NE of Carlisle

This rather remote village is famous for the remarkable **Bewcastle Cross**, an exceptionally well preserved carved 7th-c. cross, missing only its head, which stands in the churchyard of *St Cuthbert's Church*. The architectural historian, the late Sir Niklaus Pevsner, comments that this cross and a similar one across the Scottish border at Ruthwell have no rival for perfection for this date in the whole of Europe. The church is Victorian-Gothic with some original Norman work and a Georgian W tower; church and village stand at the edge of the windswept Bewcastle Fells. Little remains of the Roman *fort* on which the village stands; the *castle* is a mere remnant.

Overleaf: Tarn Hows

Black Combe A4

Fell at SW extremity of Lake District, NW of Millom

This great hump of a fell sits close to the sea to the SW, a landmark for passing ships. Its rock is Skiddaw Slate, an isolated portion from an arc of rock sweeping W from Skiddaw and under the sea. Its summit (1970ft) is easily reached by good paths from *Whicham* to the S, or *Bootle* to the NW. The view is superb. Wordsworth was suitably impressed:

'This Height a ministering angel might select:

Far from the summit of BLACK COMB (dread name

Derived from clouds and storms!) the amplest range

Of unobstructed prospect may be seen That British ground commands...'

(View from the Top of Black Comb)

The Isle of Man seems very close. The high fells of the Lake District are ranged to the N, and on exceptionally clear days both Scotland and Wales can be seen. Footpaths to the summit lead from the A595 near *Silcroft* or *Bootle*.

Blencathra B2

Fell off A66, NE of Keswick

Travelling N towards Keswick from Thirlmere on the A591, and approaching Thirlspot, a large dark angular mountain is seen at the head of St. John's-in-the-Vale. Its shape is distinctive. The ridge lines are unbroken, and curve up to three peaks. This, with a clean-lined forward buttress, suggests draped cloth – the effect looks rather like a colossal Bedouin tent. Blencathra, otherwise named 'Saddleback' owing to its shape suggested from other viewpoints, is an impressive hulk easily deluding sightseers into the belief that its height is well above its 2847ft. Geologically it is one with its neighbour Skiddaw. The rock is generally shaley, and breaks down into small fragments.

There are several ascent lines from the village of *Threlkeld*. Experienced scramblers prefer the ascent from *Scales via Sharp Edge*, a slim arête running to the summit. The view from the summit is superb, taking in much of the Lake District's high land.

Bootle A3

Village on A595, 6m S of Ravenglass

Bootle consists of two small villages, the old on the roadside, the new by the railway station 1m NW. 1m further W is a very good little beach, spoiled, unless volunteers have been there recently, by debris washed in from the sea. *St Michael's Church* in the old village, largely 19th-c., stands on the site of an earlier building. There are few monumental brasses in Cumbria, but here is one to Sir Hugh Askew (1562).

SE of the village rises *Black Combe* (1970ft) the Lake District's most southwesterly fell. Dominating the area, it gives splendid views of sea and fell.

Borrowdale B2/B3

Dale and villages extending 7m S of Keswick. Nat Park Inf Centre (Seatoller): Tel (059684) 294

Tourists, sight-seeing in Borrowdale in earlier days, might be warned by their coachman to keep their voices down lest the reverberations of sound should bring the crags falling down about their heads. The rough, exciting scenery had that effect. Nowadays we are less easily frightened, but we can still be awestruck at the sight of the steep crags, boulder-strewn valley, falling water, swift river, and the still water of Derwent Water, and everywhere green in summer, gold in autumn; for the Borrowdale broadleaved woodlands, sometimes apparently clinging in profusion to the rock face, are famous.

Borrowdale's scenery changes at every turn, from level lake to rough fell land around Seathwaite, and up to the highest land in England. Travelling upvalley from the E side of *Derwent Water* at the point where the road nears the lakeshore, *Great Wood* (NT) is on the left. The informal car park in the wood is the starting point for many walks, particularly the ascent of *Walla Crag*. Two other renowned lakeside beauty spots are *Ashness Bridge* (see *Watendlath*, also *Walk 7, p.32*) and **Lodore Falls** (*Walk 6, p.31*) Access to the falls is from the lake head behind *The Lodore Hotel*, on payment of a small charge. The great volume of water comes down the fell wall in a number of drops, the main one being about 90ft. Southey described the falls in his popular *Poem for Children*. After prolonged rain the falls should not be missed. Just up-valley is *Shepherd's Crag*, very popular with rock climbers. Best view of the crag is from the path going W across the marshes to the lake head.

The settlement of *Grange-in-Borrowdale* is approached further on by a stone bridge over the Derwent. Here was a grainstore when the valley was partly owned by Furness Abbey; some parts of the valley were owned by Fountains Abbey, and there were some un-Christian disputes. Up-valley again there are car parks in the tree-clad quarry heaps of *Quay Foot* (NT), and approached by a track from here is the famous *Bowder Stone*, a huge boulder which seems to be balanced on a fine point. An ascent can be made by ladder. It is arguable whether the rock fell from the crags above, or was left here by retreating ice during the Ice Age when the valley was carved out. *Castle Crag* looms high above the W bank some way up the valley. The banks and ditches on its summit are thought to be the remains of a Romano-British defence-point in a strategic position commanding a view of the valley routes (the rough approach to the castle is from Grange).

The hamlet of Rosthwaite is then reached; the National Trust owns extensive fell and woodland around this, and all the other, remote hamlets between here and the head of the valley. To the NE, tracks lead to *Watendlath; to the SE, from *Stonethwaite*, are paths to Grasmere and Langdale. To the SW is *Seatoller*, where there is a National Park Information Centre, and from here the main road goes W for *Honister Pass, but a narrow road goes onwards to *Seathwaite*, the starting-point for many of the very popular paths to the high fells. *Seathwaite Fell* due S is reputed to be the wettest place in England, with falls averaging 131in. It is certainly the wettest place with a rain gauge. Beyond Seathwaite Fell are the mountain tarns of *Styhead* and *Sprinkling*. Surrounded by the high, craggy fells, Styhead is at

the great crossroads of mountain paths going onwards to Wasdale Head, NW for Great Gable, S for the Scafells and SE for Langdale and Eskdale.

Borrowdale was the home of Sir Hugh Walpole (d. 1941) whose *Herries Chronicle*, the saga of a Lakeland family, is set in the area.

Bow Fell   B3
Mountain W of B5343 at head of Great Langdale

Bow Fell (2960ft), stands close to the centre of the great hub of the central fells in the Borrowdale Volcanic Series, at the W end of Langdale and the NE end of Eskdale. Seen from Langdale, it is a peak with a long lower ridge running N from it. From Eskdale to the S Bow Fell looks conical, like a child's drawing of a mountain. There are some popular rock climbs on the E face. The best known walkers' route to the summit is from *Stool End Farm* in Langdale up the approach rib known as *The Band*, some 3¼m, with a 2640ft ascent. It has a true mountaineers' top, rugged and interesting. The splendid summit views are all of the central mountains, though the the Pennines are visible to the E beyond Windermere.

Bowness-on-Solway   B1
Village off B5307, 14m W of Carlisle

Bowness has the distinct flavour of a border town. It seems almost possible to lob a stone into Scotland across the Solway marshes, and anciently, when it was England's turn to settle differences, the villagers could watch Annan burn (as in 1547). Bowness is built of Roman stones, for the village stands on the W outpost of *Hadrian's Wall* and inside what was the Roman fort of Maia. On the side of *The King's Arms Hotel* the brewery have thoughtfully provided a plan of the fort. It used to be assumed that the Wall finished at Bowness, but traces have been found of defensive ditches to the W. Pottery finds in one, 1½m W, dates the ditch to the Wall-building period. *St Michael's Church* has Norman doorways and a fine Norman font.

Bowness-on-Windermere   C3(A)
Village on A592, on E side of Windermere. Inf
(in season): Tel (09662) 5602. Nat Park Inf Centre:
Tel (09662) 2895

At the beginning of the last century Wordsworth was worrying about the changes in Bowness brought about by tourism and the new land-buying aristocracy. Cynics might say that it has long since become a victim of its own popularity. Yet, crowds and occasional traffic jams aside, there is nothing ugly in the village. Firm palnning has ensured that there are no amusement arcades, or otherwise garish and incongruous commercial developments.

Bowness, of course, is a major tourist honeypot with a strong regular following. The boat landings, the steamer pier and the promenade, with their elegant views across the water to the tree-clad islands and the heights on the W shore, are the great and obvious attractions. There is lake shore access at *Cockshott Point*, to the SW, to the car ferry which links the village to the Hawkshead road. Popular sights on this route include Beatrix Potter's home at *Near Sawrey*. The sealink 'steamers' run a regular service in season from Bowness pier to Waterhead in the N, and Lakeside in the S. Smaller passenger boats run tours, and boats can be hired.

The shopping street of Bowness runs steeply up to *Windermere* town with no obvius boundary. Most of the substantial buildings are of mid-19th-c. **St Martin's Church** is worth a visit, to see its quaint painted decorations and

Windermere

verses (16th-c. and Victorian). There is a fine carving of St Martin and the Beggar, and some 15th-c. stained glass thought to h ave been 'borrowed' from *Cartmel Priory*. There is an Information Centre and Theatre (NP) on the promenade, and nearby is the modernistic *Royal Windermere Yacht Club*. **Windermere Steam Boat Museum** is on Rayrigg Road (A592), ½m N of the village. It has Victorian and Edwardian steamboats, and other vintage craft.

Brampton
C1
Small town on A69, 9m NE of Carlisle. EC Thur MD Wed. Inf (in season): Tel (06977) 3433

Brampton is an exceptionally attractive town with a fine old Market Place. It awaits patiently the by-pass which will take the heavy traffic even further away from its precincts. In the Market Place is the Georgian *Moot House* (1817), and other handsome Georgian buildings line the Main Street which runs between the Market Place and *St Martin's Church*. The church, a Victorian extravaganza of styles, caused a stir in English architectural circles when it was completed in 1874. It has stained glass by William Morris and Sir Edward Burne-Jones. The remains of the *Old Church* stand 1m to the W, on the site of a Roman fort near *Hadrian's Wall*.

Talkin Tarn, a Country Park with boating facilities (no power boats), is to the S, and *Lanercost Priory* is 2½m NE of the town.

Brantwood
B3(B)

Historic house off B5285 on E bank of Coniston Water, 3m SE of Coniston village

John Ruskin, writer, artist and philosopher, had a powerful influence on Victorian attitudes to art and politics. His eloquence, his critical faculty and his appeal to the best in human nature were irresistible. He was a giant of his time. He made Brantwood, on the E side of Coniston Water, his home from 1872 until his death in 1900. He bought it as a 'small place' from William Linton, a wood engraver and magazine editor, and added to it over the years. Ruskin loved the across-lake views from the house, and from the grounds where he laid out paths, and had a seat made for himself near a waterfall. A *Nature Trail* leads through the grounds.

The house was acquired in 1932 by J. Howard Whitehouse, who collected many of the treasures now on view here (by appointment only). These include pictures of Ruskin and his contemporaries, and some of his furniture.

Brockhole (NP)
C3(A)

Nat Park Visitor Centre off A591, 2½m NW of Windermere town. Inf: Tel (09662) 2231

In 1898 a Manchester industrialist, Henry Gaddum, built a house for himself on the shores of Windermere. This was Brockhole, which later became a convalescent home and since 1969 has been the property of the Lake District National Park Authority. It is used imaginatively, and fulfils its statutory duty to educate and inform the public on all aspects of the National Park. There are displays, special events and courses, and regular programmes of lectures on geology, natural history, literary associations and farming. The 30 acres of attractive grounds extend to the shore with plenty of room for picnics as well as for a large car park, a *Nature Trail*, and a beautifully kept garden.

Brothers Water (NT)
C2

Lake beside A592, 1½m S of Patterdale

Brothers Water is a small, seemingly straight-edged lake whose beauty catches the eye on the descent of *Kirkstone Pass* towards Patterdale and Ullswater. Wordsworth suggested that the old name for it was 'Broader Water', but that it was given its present name following a tragic fatal accident to two brothers who were skating here in the 19th c. There is a pleasant walk along the W bank on a public right of way.

Brough
D3

Village on A66 (A685), 8m SE of Appleby. Event: Hill Fair (Sep 30). EC Thur. Inf: Tel (09304) 260

The ruin of the Norman **Brough Castle** dominates the village of Brough. It stands on the site of the Roman fort of Verterae, and dates from the 11th c. The Scots took it in the English incursions of 1174, but it was strengthened by Robert de Vipont, and although the village was burned in further Scots raids the castle remained unbreached. In the Wars of the Roses it was held by Lord Clifford, a Lancastrian, but he was killed and the castle was taken by Warwick the Kingmaker. It was restored to the Cliffords by the Tudors. The castle suffered an accidental fire in the 16th c. and was restored by Lady Anne Clifford; in 1666 another fire engulfed it. Now in care of the DoE, the *Keep*, *SE Tower* and *Gatehouse* make an imposing sight. Fragments of 11th-c. brickwork are still visible in the curtain wall. Nearby, *St Michael's Church* dates from the 12th c. and retains some medieval features, in spite of Scottish vandalism. The gypsies' annual horse fair recalls Brough's days as a coaching centre.

Brougham
C2

Historic castle ruin and chapel on A66 (M6) 1m SE of Penrith

Brougham stands by the crossroads of the M6/A6 going N and S, and the A66 going W to E across the Pennines. These modern routes follow the very ancient ones. The Romans recognised the strategic importance of the ancient British road junction and built a fort, Brocavum, then cunningly protected by the confluence of the Rivers Lowther and Eamont. It accommodated up to a thousand infantry and cavalry. Now only the foundations can be seen, as the stone was 'quarried' to build the Norman **Castle** on the banks of the River Eamont. The very impressive ruins are protected by the DoE.

Brougham was won from Scottish control by Henry II, and Gospatrick, son of Orm, built a keep here in the 12th c. Later as the castle came into Vipont hands, and by marriage to the influential Clifford family, it was extended and improved. A great chamber was built by the keep in the 13th c., and a great hall S of this. Across the courtyard SW of the keep are the ruins of the 13th-c. servants' quarters; the chapel block next to it was built around the 14th c. The SW tower is late 13th-c. The last work was done by the great restorer of the Cliffords' northern properties, Lady Anne Clifford, in the 17th c. Ruination came after 1714, when Lady Anne's successors allowed the castle to be stripped of lead and timber.

Lady Anne had much to do with the restoration in the 17th c. of the quietly sited little Chapel of Ninekirks, otherwise **St Wilfrid's**, by a minor road 1m SW of the castle. Masons' marks suggest that the chapel was built substantially on the site of an earlier chapel by the 14th-c. castle builders. In 1840 more restoration was done; the interesting profusion of woodwork now to be seen was brought from France by Lord William Brougham, and cut to fit by local workmen. It is mainly 15th-c., but the pulpit is 16th-c. There is some 14th and 16th-c. glass in the E window. A beautiful 15th-c. Flemish triptych was removed for restoration in 1968, and is now housed in Carlisle Cathedral.

The *Countess Pillar* is ½m E of the castle by the A66. This was erected by Lady Anne in 1654 to mark the place of her last parting with her 'good and pious mother'.

To the W are two Bronze Age monuments (see *Mayburgh*).

Broughton-in-Furness   B3
Village on A595, 9m NW of Ulverston

Until Ulverston stole its thunder by linking itself by canal to the sea (1847), Broughton-in-Furness was an important market town serving a wide area of Furness. It still has its cattle market, but now it is just a friendly little unspoilt village with an impressive *Market Square*, complete with slate slab stalls and village stocks among trees. Its *Town Hall* dates from 1766. *St Mary's Church* was rebuilt in the Early English style (1873), but has a Norman S doorway. The obelisk to the town's benefactor, John Gilpin, was erected in 1810.

Nearby *Broughton Tower* (not open to the public) is an 18th-19th c. mansion built around a 14th-c. defensive tower. Scottish raiders were the problem. The tower's one-time resident, Sir Thomas Broughton, lent his support to Lambert Simnel when the claimant to the throne landed in Furness some ten miles away in 1487 with his Irish mercenaries. After Simnel's defeat, Henry VII seized the tower and lands and presented them to the Stanleys. They were later sold to the Sawrey family.

The woodlands around Broughton provided charcoal for the Furness iron industry. In the 18th c., a busy forge stood by the River Duddon 1½m to the W. The ruin, *Duddon Forge*, is open to the public on application to the National Park Authority.

Part of the Market Hall houses the **Hadwin Motor Cycle Museum**, with lovingly restored pre-war machines.

Burgh-by-Sands   B1
Village off B5307, 5m NW of Carlisle

Burgh is a border town standing on *Hadrian's Wall* and built from the stones of the Roman fort, Aballava. Scottish raids from across the Solway marshes must have been commonplace, so much so that **St Michael's Church**, with its Norman doorway, had its tower remodelled into a heavy defensive structure in the 14th c. Into this the villagers could flee on receiving warning, closing the heavy iron gate behind them. The gate is still intact.

1¼m N and approachable on foot only, along a lane, is **Edward I's Monument**. It stands by the marshes, isolated and atmospheric. 'The Hammer of the Scots' died here of old age on his way to his fourth invasion of Scotland a year after defeating Robert the Bruce in 1306. The pillar was erected in 1685, and rebuilt and restored twice in the 19th c. Another effort is about due.

Buttermere (NT) B2
Lake beside B5289, SW of Keswick

In tourism's early days Buttermere was rated highly for its beauty. Nothing has changed here. Improved access to other attractions has increased their popularity; Buttermere is protected from the Keswick approaches by two passes, *Honister Pass* E from Borrowdale, and *Newlands* NE from Braithwaite, often impassable in winter. The mile-long lake of pure water, sometimes inexplicably green, is a delight. The triple peaks of High Stile, High Crag, and Red Pike are the backcloth to the view from the road. It is possible to walk round the lake by public paths (see *Walk 4*, p.31), and *Buttermere* village, with its tiny dale church, makes a good centre for walking and climbing. One of its inns, *The Fish Inn*, was the scene of an early 19th-c. melodrama when the landlord's daughter married a bigamist, who was tried and hanged soon after. Wordsworth was one of many who described the affair. The village stands N of the lake on the B5289 from Cockermouth.

Caldbeck B2
Village on B5299, 12m S of Carlisle

Everyone 'kens' John Peel, the famous huntsman. Caldbeck was his home village. His tombstone, suitably decorated with hound and horn, is in the churchyard. Around is the country where he hunted on foot in his locally homespun 'coat so grey'. The song was composed by another Caldbeck man, John Woodcock Graves, and William Metcalf, organist at Carlisle Cathedral, provided the popular tune. The village has a quiet charm. *St Kentigern's Church* has Norman origins, but stands on a much earlier foundation. St Kentigern was a Celtic saint. The 'Maid of Buttermere', who ended her days in Caldbeck, is also buried in the churchyard.

Calder Abbey A3
Ruin off A595, ¾m E of Calder Bridge

Though not open to the public, this beautiful ruined abbey on the bank of the River Calder can be viewed from a nearby footpath. The highest detail is the remaining portion of the church tower, supported by four arches. Other parts of the church, including the N arcade of the nave, and the chapter house remain. A late Georgian private house occupies part of the site on what was the monks' frater and dormitory.

The abbey was founded in 1134, by the Lord of Copeland, as a sister to Furness Abbey. It was rather too handy for Scottish raiders. It was sacked in 1138, the monks fleeing to Furness; rebuilt, it was raided again in 1180. The new stone church was rebuilt in 1220, but again it suffered severely, in the great raid of Scottish marauders which also got as far as Furness following Bannockburn in 1322. The abbey was yet again rebuilt, and survived until the Dissolution in 1536.

Carlisle see p.52

Carrock Fell B2
Fell off minor roads (A66), N of Mungrisdale

Carrock Fell (2174ft) is an eastern spur of the Caldbeck Fells. On its summit is a ruin believed to have been a large Iron Age **hill fort**, some 736ft long and 373ft wide. The gaps in the stonework suggest that this was a stronghold of the Brigante tribe, taken and razed by the Romans.

Geologically the fell has been described as the most complex in the Lake District. Belonging to the Volcanic Series, and standing out from the sedimentary Skiddaw Slates, it is rich in minerals; over a score have been identified.

Cartmel C4
Village off B5277, 2¼m W of Grange-over-Sands.
Events: Cartmel Races (Spring & Summer Bank Hols, also Sat & Wed after 1st Mon in Aug), Cartmel Show (Wed after 1st Mon in Aug)

Cartmel's **Priory Church of St Mary the Virgin** is sometimes called 'the Cathedral of the Lakes', and in size it is certainly out of proportion to the small, very attractive village it dominates. An unusual, endearing feature is the tower, with the upper stage placed diagonally on the lower. The village is idyllic, with its little river and the village square which is, alas, too often exasperatingly filled and obscured with parked cars, even though there is a car park a few yards beyond. The 14th-c. *Priory Gatehouse* (NT), now an information centre, gives entry to the square, opposite the market cross.

The Augustinian Priory was founded by William Marshall, Earl of Pembroke, in the late 12th c. Legend has it that the monks were told in a dream to build between two watercourses, one flowing N and the other S; and so they did. The priory prospered and grew, but now there is nothing to see of its buildings except the church and gatehouse, so thorough was the demolition carried out at the Dissolution.

The church was saved from demolition when it was successfully argued that it served also as a parish church. The parishioners were allowed the S aisle of the choir; the rest of the building, its roof stripped of its lead, was left to become ruinous until in 1618 George Preston of Holker Hall enlisted local support to repair the whole church. Much later the church again fell into disrepair, but in 1859 the 7th Duke of Devonshire, again with local support, started a restoration project which was completed in 1870.

On inspection of the church, there is evidence of a long sequence of building. The main doorway, chancel and transepts are 12th-c. The inspiring Perpendicular E window, 45ft high, replaced an earlier one in the 15th c. Little is left of its original glass. The peculiar tower is of the same period, and the short nave was built afterwards. In the *choir* the carving of the stalls and misericords (15th-c.) is uncommonly fine, the latter showing some amusing originality; the excellent Flemish carved oak screen was George Preston's gift. The beautifully-sculpted Harrington Tomb, dating from the 14th c., is exceptionally

well preserved. Among other memorials are some which commemorate persons lost on the often dangerous low-tide route across the sands of Morecambe Bay.

The Cartmel Races are held on Cartmel's National Hunt Course in the fields beyond the village square during spring and summer. In August, the Cartmel Show includes show jumping and Cumrbian hound trailing.

A footpath leads from the village E up to *Hampsfell*.

Castlerigg Stone Circle (NT)   B2
Ancient site off A66/A591, E of Keswick

The Victorians called Keswick's Bronze Age stone circle the 'Druids' Circle', but we now know that such circles are centuries older than the coming of the Druids. In its superb dramatic setting, Castlerigg is unsurpassed. It stands on a platform surrounded by a ring of high fells. Looking across the circle towards Helvellyn, into changing patterns of light and shade, is a rare experience. There are 48 megalithic stones in the shape of an oval approx 100 x 109ft, with some of the stones forming a rectangle on the E side of the circle. There is no explanation for this, but the arrangement is not unknown in other circles. It has been suggested that the stones have an astronomical alignment, making it a stone calendar for the guidance of farmers.

Cat Bells   B2
Fell SW of Keswick

The origin of the name of the fell, prominent in the view as a hump over the SW end of Derwent Water, is a mystery. Cat Bells is possibly the corruption of a Celtic name. It is in an area once extensively mined. The summit of the fell, 1482ft, is a popular attraction for walkers but it can be a trap for the unwary; smooth-soled footwear on the steep slopes is a frequent cause of accidents. The views are excellent.

To its E, the fell overlooks *Brandlehow Park* which was the first piece of land to be acquired in the Lake District by the National Trust (1901).

CARLISLE

Population 101,000

Tourist Information Moot Hall.
Tel Carlisle (0228) 25517

EC Thur **MD** Wed, Sat

Events Cumberland Show (Jul);
Carlisle Great Fair (3rd week in Aug)

Places of interest
*All places listed are open to the public
and described in the text that follows*

Churches
Carlisle Cathedral

St Cuthbert's St Cuthbert's Lane

Historic Buildings
Carlisle Castle
Summer Mon-Sat 9-6.30, Sun 2-6.30
Winter Mon-Sat 9.30-4, Sun 2-4

The Guildhall Greenmarket
Open on application to Carlisle
Museum

The Citadel

Museums
Carlisle Museum and Art Gallery
Tullie House, Castle Street
Summer Mon-Fri 9-7, Sat 9-5, Sun
2.30-5 Winter Mon-Sat 9-5

Border Regiment Museum
The Castle
Summer Mon-Sat 9.30-6.30, Sun 2-
6.30 Winter Mon-Sat 9.30-4, Sun 2-4

Guildhall Museum Greenmarket
As above

Cumbria's busy cathedral city and
county town looks as modern as any
other city, with its obligatory shopping
centres, new concrete buildings, and
fiendish one-way traffic system. Many
ancient cities' histories can be read in
their stones; not Carlisle's. Carlisle was
a frontier town for 1000 frequently turbulent years, and most of its masonry,
at some time, has been disarranged with
violence, then rearranged in urgent
haste. Only parts of the squat red castle,
and of the diminished cathedral, remain
to tell the long story.

A substantial part of the old stone was
dressed by Roman masons, for here the
Emperor Hadrian's solution to the
problem of the fierce frontier tribesmen
was to build his great defensive wall to
the W along the Solway coast, through
Carlisle and across northern England.
The walls and forts later became handy
quarries. The first fort was built by Agricola, when Carlisle was the Roman
garrison town of Luguvalium, but Hadrian later built another (Petriana) across
the river. This was the largest fort on
Hadrian's Wall, and housed 1000
cavalry. St Michael's Church and other
19th-c. buildings now occupy the site.

After three centuries of occupation
the Romans left a thriving town; later
on Christianity was firmly established
following the welcome to St Cuthbert in
685. The next visitations were less
welcome. The Danes first burned,
then occupied the town, and held it
from the 9th c. When the army of William Rufus took it for the English
Crown in 1092 a new era of building
began, but this was by no means the
beginning of more settled times. The
inhabitants of both sides of the border
were a mixture of feuding, truculent
Celts and testy Danes and Vikings; and
their Norman overlords, both in
England and Scotland, were inclined to
dispute ownership. Between 1136 and
1216, which saw the founding of Carlisle's Augustinian priory and the building of the cathedral and castle, the city
and much of the county was four times
alternately Scottish and English. In
1292, the city and its cathedral were
destroyed by a fire started by a family
quarrel.

In the early 14th c. Edward I, 'the
Hammer of the Scots', used Carlisle as
his campaign garrison and held three
parliaments in the castle's Great Hall.
The King's ambition to bring Scotland
and England under common rule was
frustrated largely by the bloody
thoroughness of his military successes,
for this aroused a determination for
revenge amongst the Scots. The ban-
ner was carried by Robert the Bruce,
who after the death of Edward took

the offensive. Following his success at Bannockburn Carlisle was taken four times, though the castle held out.

By the 16th c., there was need for more rebuilding. The castle, though ruinous, was vital to the task of policing the still-troublesome border. The borderers on both sides, later romanticized in ballads, were violent, fast-moving cattle thieves ready to cheat and to change allegiances whenever it suited them. The constant feuding brought poverty to the city. Peace finally came with the union of the crowns of Scotland and England in 1603, and there was a brief period to consider repairs of an aesthetic nature: in 1639 Charles I, in a letter to the Cathedral Chapter, deplored the building's dilapidation. But the worst had yet to come.

In the Civil War Carlisle was Royalist, and in 1644 retreating troops under Sir Thomas Glenham, Commander of the North, took refuge in the castle. General Leslie's Scottish Presbyterian troops laid siege, and before the defenders surrendered they were reduced to eating rats and dogs. The castle had been damaged by bombardments and the Scots made frantic efforts to repair it, using the cathedral as a quarry. Stone was gleaned by pulling down the priory cloisters and the chapter house, and when this was not enough, even a large proportion of the cathedral's nave was removed. The castle fell again to the Royalists, and yet again received a battering, this time from naval guns brought in for the purpose. Cromwell's men regained control, and repairs were again necessary. A century later, in 1745, the city and castle fell at the Scottish rebels' surprise entry, when Bonnie Prince Charlie proclaimed his father King from the market cross. In the rebels' retreat later, the rearguard of 400 Highlanders surrendered to the Duke of Cumberland's army; both the castle and the cathedral were filled with prisoners.

In 1815 the city 'fell' again, this time to the 'improvers' who took away walls and gates, and demolished the Great Hall of the castle. As the century progressed, the city changed shape. Roads were improved, and railway lines converged on its heart. The former garrison town became a major textile centre, and the boom brought the development of the fine Georgian and Victorian terraces that are a feature of the city. Despite all these changes, Cumbria's major city retains an echo of its turbulent past. The feuding is over, but the old border family names live on and the visitor will still hear Cumbrian and Scottish dialects mingling in the market place.

Carlisle Cathedral is near the city centre. The foreshortening of the nave that resulted from the destructive quarrying is evident at first sight in the red sandstone building's awkward proportions. Originally a Norman priory church, this is the second smallest cathedral in England (only Oxford is smaller).

On entering the cathedral, however, the beauty of the *E window* seizes the eye: it is 15ft high, with delicate tracery. The outer walls of the chancel are 13th-c., but the arcade piers were replaced after the fire of 1292. The capitals are decorated with leaves and small figures representing the months of the year. The *choir* dates from the 14th c. The misericords are amusing and lively, with carvings of birds, dragons, angels, a mermaid, fox and goose. There is further 15th-c. comic-strip story-telling on the back of the choir stalls, showing the legend of St Cuthbert and St Anthony and the Apostles. At this time, the whole of the cathedral would have been colourfully painted. The chancel ceiling is a good example, but this lovely design of stars in a blue sky, by Owen Jones, dates from the 1850s. In the floor of the E end of the choir is a notable brass memorial to Bishop Richard Bell (1495). Above the altar in the *N transept* is a beautifully made Flemish *triptych* of the early 16th c., brought here from Brougham Chapel for safe-keeping. In the W wall of the *S transept* is an odd piece of 12th-c. graffito. The script reads, 'Tolfihu wrote these runes on this stone'.

Of the rest of the priory little remains; but the 15th-c. *Frater* stands to its full height. The *Undercroft* is 14th-c. and is now open as a café and a bookshop. On the S side, against the W walls of the priory grounds, is the *Deanery*. This is essentially a 12th-c. pele tower with 16th-c. restorations. There is public access to the *Prior's Room*, with its remarkable ceiling restored in 1976. The *Gatehouse* to the priory grounds is 16th-c. At the end of the grounds, near Abbey Street, is the longest surviving section of the old *city wall*.

Leaving the priory area by the gatehouse, Abbey Street leads to Tullie House, Carlisle's **Museum and Art Gallery**. Built in 1689 as a grand residence, it has fine 19th-c. extensions. The museum houses a comprehensive collection of Roman stonework with sculptures and inscriptions, altars (mostly from Hadrian's Wall), Roman jewellery, and other domestic and military items. There are rooms with displays of natural history, costume, toys and dolls, and there is a good representative collection of English porcelain. All is well arranged, in a friendly atmosphere. The art gallery has some notable pre-Raphaelites including works by Ford Madox Brown, Arthur Hayes and D.G. Rossetti. There is a library, and regular special exhibitions.

Carlisle Castle The red sandstone castle is approached from Castle Street, E of the museum, by an underpass beneath the inner ring road. On the left is a remnant of the *city wall*, and *Richard of Gloucester's Tower*, or *Tile Tower*. Richard was here to police the borders as Warden of the Marches in the 15th c. and his crest, a white boar, is carved high on the tower.

The castle ditch originally held water, and was stocked with fish: entry is by the bridge, once of course a drawbridge. This was protected by *William de Ireby's Tower*, three storeys high. The square *barbican* is covered by the presence of arrow slits in the parapet

above. The castle's outer bailey is now occupied by a modern army barracks. The inner ward on the right was protected by another water-filled ditch, and its drawbridge, in turn, was protected by the 14th-c. *Captain's Tower*: a warm reception was guaranteed for unwelcome guests, there being slits in the passage roof for pouring boiling oil. Further protection was provided by a portcullis and two heavy doors.

The great *Keep* dominates the inner ward: entry to this, too, was barred by a portcullis. The earliest part of the castle (dating from the 12th c.), this building shows much evidence of repair over the centuries; an exhibition on the ground floor illustrates the city's defences since 1092. On the second floor the *window embrasure*, formerly secured by a heavy door, was once a prison cell. A wall here is covered in carvings executed by prisoners in the 14th and 15th c. There are knights in armour, dragons, mermaids, and religious motifs. The roof of the keep makes an excellent viewpoint.

The **Border Regiment Museum** is housed in *Queen Mary's Tower*. The display includes uniforms, weapons and trophies from 1702.

Running parallel with the Georgian *Castle Street*, back to the city centre, is Fisher Street. At the city end is the cast-iron and glass-covered *Market*. This is real Carlisle: nothing like the standard supermarket. There are small, individually owned stalls, a warm friendly atmosphere, personal service, and time to chat with fellow shoppers and shopkeepers. It is an institution.

In the market is the 14th-c. **Guildhall**, now a small museum featuring the old trades guilds. The upper floors are timber-framed. Across the way is the *Moot Hall* or Town Hall, the present building dating from the 18th c. It houses the *Tourist Information Centre*. In front is the *Market Cross* (1682), a tall column surmounted by a sundial. Here in 1745 Charles Stuart proclaimed his father King after the Highlanders had taken the city. Opposite the cross, St Cuthbert's Lane leads to the parish

Carlisle Castle

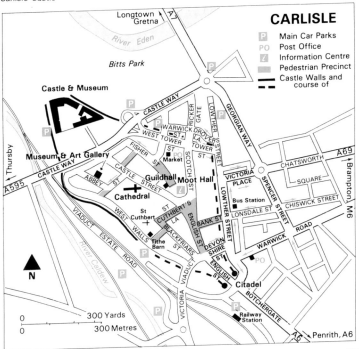

church of **St Cuthbert**. This handsome 18th-c. church stands just S of the cathedral, and occupies the site of a chapel built in 685, after the Saint had visited the community. Blackfriars Street leads SE from here into English Street and thence to the *Citadel*, once the defensive gateway to the city. The original arrangement was built in Henry VIII's reign by a German military engineer, and it consists of a wall and gateway standing between two towers. Alterations in 1807 included a partial demolition, and the W tower was moved further W to allow room for the Law Courts.

Enthusiasts for Victorian architecture will enjoy the *Railway Station* in mock-Tudor. This station was shared by no less than six railway companies in 1846. They amalgamated and became two, the LMS and LNER, in 1923. *The County Hotel* nearby is a fine example of Anthony Salvin's work.

Carlisle Great Fair takes place at the end of August. A revival of the traditional fair, its events include music, dancing and processions, and the Proclamation of the Fair Charter takes place in front of the Town Hall. An open market is held in the city centre, with stallholders in period costume. The Cumberland Show in July is a major agricultural show, with traditional and modern events.

5m E of Carlisle off the B6263 are **Corby Castle Gardens**. In the grounds of the old mansion (not open), they include fine woodland and attractive walks laid out along the River Eden in the 18th c. Also a summerhouse, fish traps and caves.

5m NW of Carlisle is **Burgh-by-Sands*, where Edward I died on his march to Scotland against Robert the Bruce.

Cockermouth

Town off A66, 13m W of Keswick. Event: Cockermouth Show (Sat before 1st Sun in Aug). EC Thur MD Mon. Inf (in season): Tel (0900) 822634

The A66 may have damaged Bassenthwaite but it has been a blessing to Cockermouth, for heavy traffic no longer bowls through the narrows and into the main street. The wide, tree-lined main street is a pleasant feature. Its open markets and fairs are no more, but Cockermouth remains a busy market town serving a wide area. At the W end of the main street is **Wordsworth's House** (NT), the 18th-c. town house where the poet was born (1770). It contains a small audio-visual display, and has an adjoining shop. Sir Niklaus Pevsner called the building, which still retains its original panelling, staircases and fireplaces, 'quite a swagger house for such a town'. Wordsworth is commemorated in a stained-glass window in the large Victorian *Church of All Saints*, S of the market place.

Another handsome building, *Lorton Hall*, stands near the River Cocker about 3½m SE of the town. This is a 17th-c. house built on to a pele tower; the medieval and the classical styles of building make an interesting contrast, characteristic of the region's grand houses. The Hall may be viewed by appointment.

At *Papcastle*, 1m NW of the town, the Roman fort of Derventio stood on a road from Carlisle to the NE. It is now hardly visible. Derventio was a large cavalry fort, no doubt serving as a quick-response back-up to the Solway and W coast defences. The *Castle* (not normally open to the public), stands on the E side of town between the Rivers Derwent and Cocker. The first structure was built in 1134 by Waltheof, Earl of Dunbar, when Cockermouth belonged to Scotland. William de Fortibus carted stone from the Roman fort to rebuild and strengthen the castle from the mid-13th c. Only the lower masonry survives from this date, the rest of the building, the gatehouses and the kitchen tower, being substantially 14th-c.

The castle has seen a great deal of action. First came the Scottish raids (sometimes assisted by English opportunists), lasting until Union with England in the early 17th c. In the Wars of the Roses it was held by Lancastrians, and taken by Yorkists. In the

Civil War the castle was besieged for two months by Royalists, under Sir William Huddleston, until relieved by Parliamentarian troops from Lancashire. Afterwards the castle fell into disrepair until its restoration by General Wyndham in the 19th c.

A local genius was John Dalton, born of a Quaker family at nearby Eaglesfield in 1766. He was a schoolmaster at the age of 13; his famous papers on the atomic theory were published between 1802 and 1804. A local reprobate, or perhaps hero, was Fletcher Christian, who led the Mutiny on the *Bounty*. He was born at Moorland Close in 1764, and attended the grammar school where Wordsworth was a pupil, which once stood in the churchyard.

The Cockermouth Show is a Cumbrian agricultural show; produce and crafts are displayed. Hound trailing and Cumberland or Westmorland wrestling are among the major events.

4m W of Cockermouth to the S of the A66 is **Wythop Mill** a water-powered sawmill (open summer only) with an exhibition of wood-working machinery and other rural crafts.

Colwith Falls (NT) B3(A)
Waterfall W of Ambleside

Colwith is at the foot of *Little Langdale*. The **waterfall** is approached by a footpath just S of Colwith Bridge on the left of the minor road. The footpath is on NT land, and care is needed as one nears the ravine where the River Brathay, flowing E from Little Langdale Tarn, drops about 46ft into a pool before turning N to join Elter Water.

Conishead Priory B4
Historic house on A5087, 2m S of Ulverston

Conishead Priory was an Augustinian hospital founded in the 12th c., later receiving priory status. One of its charges was to provide a guide to lead travellers over the treacherous sands of Morecambe Bay, to and from the Lancaster side. *Chapel Island*, a small island off-shore from Conishead, had a small chapel as a safe staging post.

Following the Dissolution, and the disposal and dismantling of the Priory, grant of the lands went to William Stanley, second Lord Monteagle, who built a house here. In the mid-17th c. it passed to the Braddyll family, and in 1818 Colonel Thomas Braddyll found the house in such disrepair that he commissioned a complete rebuilding. The architect was Philip Wyatt, son of James Wyatt; no expense was spared. In 1840, after a disastrous speculation, Colonel Braddyll was forced to sell the estate. The house became an hotel; in the 1930s it became a miners' convalescent home; then it stood empty. In 1976 the estate was bought for use as a residential college for Buddhist studies. Faced with dry rot and leaking roofs, the new owners have embarked on a mammoth task of restoration.

The house is built in an elaborate late Gothic style. The entrance through a *Gatehouse* flanked with high towers opens onto a large hall, with a high ribbed-vaulted ceiling; ornate plaster ceilings are also a notable feature. A gallery at first-floor level has a 16th-c. oak screen brought from Samlesbury Hall near Preston, and the *Oak Room* has some beautifully carved woodwork, also brought from Samlesbury.

The house and grounds have been opened up to help raise revenue for restoration. The *Grounds* extend to 70 acres, and a very good nature trail has been laid out. There are regular guided tours, and there is an audio-visual presentation.

Coniston B3(B)
Village on A593, 7m S of Ambleside. EC Wed.
Inf (in season): Tel (09664) 533

Coniston has earned its living from mining and quarrying for centuries. The quarrying survives for the slate, a 'tuff' formed from fine volcanic material which is decorative and very hard. It can be highly polished, and in this state is used for facing buildings all over the world. But Coniston has also long been a popular holiday centre, increasingly so after the coming of the railway in 1859. The line has now gone, and with it one of the most picturesque journeys in the country.

John Ruskin lived across Coniston Water at *Brantwood for 28 years, and his monument, carved from local stone to an elaborate design by W. Collingwood, is in the churchyard. The **Ruskin Museum** contains many items relating to Ruskin, among them his fine collection of mineral specimens.

On the village green is a *memorial* to Donald Campbell, killed on the lake in 1967 while attempting to break the world water speed record. The boat landings, where boats can be hired, are reached by a road and track on the S side of the bridge, and the same road leads to a footpath going SW from a bridge past Coniston's oldest building, a 16th-c. farmhouse, *Coniston Hall* (NT). Thence a footpath follows the shore along 3m of lakeside land.

Coniston Old Man   B3(B)
Mountain W of Coniston village

The Coniston Old Man range covers some 21 sq m, reaching a highest point of 2635ft where the 'Man', a stone summit cairn, stands. The mountain is in the Borrowdale Volcanic Series.

The other main peaks all exceed 2500ft. On the buttresses and ravines of *Dow Crag* to the W, the sport of rock climbing was pioneered. It stands behind *Goats Water*, a tarn whose levels make the soaring cliffs all the more awesome by contrast. *Brim Fell* is just N of the Old Man, and further N are the peaks of *Swirl How* and *Great Carrs*. *Grey Friars* rises to the NW and to the NE is *Wetherlam*. At 2502ft this mountain is the lowest in height but certainly not in bulk; it is prominent in views from the NE, and particularly over Windermere.

Coniston Old Man is seen in its imposing entirety from the gentle slopes of the Silurian Series of rocks on the E side of Coniston Water, particularly from *Brantwood, John Ruskin's old home. The mountainside is riddled with abandoned mine holes and scarred with quarries. The mines, probably active since Roman times and once so prosperous, are now all closed: two quarries are still productive.

The Old Man is crossed S of Dow by an old road (impassable to cars), the *Walna Scar*. This makes a good ascent route to the summit from Coniston; but the most popular route is by old quarry tracks past *Low Water*, with a scramble to the finish. Another very popular route is by *Church Beck* and *Coppermines Valley*, and alongside *Levers Water*, another of the mountain's tarns. Although not high, the fell can be dangerous in bad weather. Casualties are collected by volunteers from the local Mountain Rescue Team.

Coniston Water   B3(B)
Lake E of A593, SE of Coniston village

In 1196 Coniston Water was *Thorstanes Watter*, the name originating from its owner Thorstein, one of the district's Viking settlers. It is the third largest lake in the Lake District, and like its larger sisters has always been a highway. Once, ore from the mines and slate from the quarries were barged down the lake, and at other periods between the 11th and 17th c. iron ore was brought up the lake to be smelted at lake-shore 'bloomeries', where wood for charcoal-making was in good supply. When the railway came to Coniston in 1859, the railway company set up a steamer service on the lake. Two boats were in use and one survives, the *Gondola*, an iron steam ship of elegant design. Having been restored by the National Trust, it is now in service again.

In 1967, Donald Campbell attempted to break the world speed record on water on Coniston. While doing an estimated 320 mph, his boat pitched over and broke up. This occurred at a deep part of the lake (145ft), and Campbell's body and the bulk of the wreckage were never recovered. There is a memorial to Campbell in *Coniston* village.

A narrow public road runs down the E side of Coniston. On the W, much of the shore is accessible by a public path and over land owned by the National Park Authority. Power boats are permitted on the lake, but there is a speed limit of 10mph. There are launching facilities at *Coniston Boating Centre*, SE of the village, but craft that can be man-handled can be launched at *Monk Coniston* to the NE of the lake, or at *Brown How* on the SW. The lake is fished for char, trout, perch and pike.

Crosby Ravensworth
D2
Village off B6260 (A66 or M6), 8½m SW of Appleby

A pretty village in need of some caring hands. **St Lawrence's Church**, sur-rounded by trees, is the imposing fea-ture. The church was built to replace a wooden structure early in the 12th c., and it came into the care of Whitby Abbey. Like other buildings in the area, it was destroyed by Scottish raid-ers. The village belonged to Scotland at the end of the 12th and the beginning of the 13th c., and the church was then re-built; work of the latter period can be seen in the six piers of the nave.

In the 15th c. Sir Lancelot Threlkeld removed the transepts and constructed the W tower. So it was until the 19th c., when George Gibson commissioned Robert Smirke (then building Lowther Castle) to make further restorations in the Gothic style. Later, J.S. Crowther contributed 'Early English' features; a vestry was added, and two chapels, and the roof was raised. In the N chapel a large tomb chest is said to be the resting place of Sir Lancelot Threlkeld.

1½m SW is **Ewe Close**, the remains of one of the most important excavated Romano-British settlements in north-ern England. It was a walled village of 1¼ acres, with outlying walled fields. The surviving village walls are 6ft high. It is suggested that the settlement was there when the Roman road from Lancaster to Carlisle was constructed, as the road curved towards it. There are remains of other settlements in the district.

Cross Fell
D2
Fell NE of Penrith

At 2930ft Cross Fell is the highest point in the Pennines, which flank the Lake District's E boundary, the Eden Valley. The fell is known for an unusual phenomenon, the 'Helm Wind'. This occurs when strong NE winds are stir-red into violent turbulence by the peculiar configuration of the fell, pro-ducing damaging gales in limited localities while other areas are in calm.

The fell is part of the Whin Sill, formed when volcanic lava forced its way horizontally along the bedding planes of sedimentary rock, protecting the softer rock below from subsequent erosion. The Whin Sill continues through Northumberland to the E coast, and the Roman Emperor Had-rian built his wall on it.

The *Pennine Way*, on its journey N, climbs to the summit of Cross Fell before continuing N across Alston Moor towards Alston and thence Hadrian's Wall.

Crosthwaite see *Keswick*

Crummock Water (NT)
B2
Lake beside B5289, SW of Keswick

Crummock Water is over twice the size of Buttermere, and shares the same val-ley. It is walled by the fells of Mellbreak (1676ft) to the W, and Grassmoor (2791ft) to the E. Crummock and Buttermere were once one, scooped out by the same glacier at the end of the Ice Age, but the massive erosion which followed before the earth was stabilized by vegetation caused the two lakes to be separated by an alluvial plain.

Crummock enjoys a quiet and remote atmosphere, although a minor road, the B5289, runs along the E side. One of the lake's feeders is *Scale Beck* to the SW, which falls rapidly down a ravine from Gale Fell, finishing with a 60ft fall, *Scale Force* (NT) the highest waterfall in the Lake District. It is possible to walk round the lake, though the W side is rough and wet.

Crummock is a clear lake, 144ft at its deepest, and holds trout, char, pike and perch. The lake is owned by the National Trust. Powered boats are not allowed on the lake, but light craft can be launched from the side of the B5289. A permit is obtainable for a small charge from Rannerdale Farm.

59

Dacre
Village off A66, 3m NW of Pooley Bridge   C2

Dacre is thought to be the site of the Anglo-Saxon Monastery mentioned by Bede ('Dacore'). Excavations in the churchyard have confirmed the existence of pre-Norman drains and walls. In 926 (according to William of Malmesbury) the three Kings Athelstan, Constantine and Owain met here to sign a peace treaty remembered as 'The Peace of Dacre'. The present Norman **St Andrew's Church** has 12th and 13th-c. features. There are two portions of cross shafts which also indicate a pre-Norman presence; one is thought to be 9th-c. and one 10th. They have unusual carvings of figures, one of which could depict the signing of the peace treaty. The four stone bears of unknown age or origin at the corners of the churchyard are a puzzle, and they appear to tell a story. Bear one, on the NW, is leaning on a 'ragged staff'; bear two is attacked by a cat which has landed on its back; bear three has reached back and grabbed the cat; bear four is eating it…

Dacre Castle is close to the church, and looks impressive. It is essentially a 14th-c. pele tower, but it was restored when in possession of the Earl of Sussex in the 17th c. The Earls of Dacre were men to be reckoned with in the wheeling and dealing, deceit and violence of the borders of the Western Marches.

Dalemain, 1m NE, is a Georgian house built onto a pele tower.

Dalemain
Historic house off A592, 3m SW of Penrith   C2

A house extended from a 12th-c. pele tower, originally in the possession of John de Morville, brother of Hugh de Morville, one of the four knights who murdered Thomas à Becket in 1172. It has been in the possession of the Hasell family since 1680.

Outside, the most striking feature is the early Georgian front of pink sandstone. Inside, there is a sharp contrast between the gracious 18th-c. atmosphere downstairs (note particularly the elegant *Chinese Drawing Room*) and the dark oak Jacobean panelling on the first floor. Of special interest here is the *Housekeeper's Room*, fully furnished and equipped with Victorian and Edwardian china and utensils, with a feeling that the housekeeper has only just left. The tower contains the **Westmorland and Cumberland Yeomanry Museum** with regimental relics. The *Old Hall* is now a tearoom.

In the courtyard is a 16th-c. barn converted to house a collection of bygone farming equipment, the **Dalemain Agricultural Museum**. Another building houses a *Countryside Museum*. The house and grounds make a pleasant place to spend a leisurely afternoon.

Dacre, 1m SW, has an interesting Norman church on a Saxon site, and a medieval castle ruin.

Dalton-in-Furness
Pop 11,000. 5m SW of Ulverston (A590/A595)   B4

Dalton was once an important market town, and the monks of Furness Abbey held courts here. The heavy square defensive tower at the end of the main street, **Dalton Castle** (NT), was built by the abbot in the 14th c. as a defence against Scots raids. After the Dissolution, Henry VIII ordered the tower to be repaired with stone from the abbey. Courts were still held here until early this century, and up to the 18th c. the tower served as a prison. It faces the friendly market place, which is overlooked by *St Mary's Church* (1882), grandly built in the Decorated style.

The town declined after the Dissolution, but it enjoyed prosperity during the 19th c. through the rapid growth of the iron industry following the discovery of iron ore. Some 7 million tons of ore were raised from mines in the area. The market lost out to *Ulverston* when that town was developed as a port in the 18th c., and then to *Barrow-in-Furness*, only 3½m away, after that town's rapid growth in the 19th c.

George Romney (1734-1802), the celebrated portrait painter, was a local man and is buried in the churchyard under a stone marked simply 'Pictor Celeberrimus'.

Derwent Water
B2
Lake beside B5289, ½m SW of Keswick

Derwent Water is Keswick's great attraction and is second only to Windermere in popularity, although it avoids the larger lake's bustle and noise (a 10mph speed limit operates). Its surrounding scenery, too, is more dramatic, and can be no more impressive than when viewed from Friar's Crag (see *Keswick*) with the high hills to the W, the crag walls to the E, and the Jaws of Borrowdale ahead. It is well-wooded, and the colour changes in spring and autumn are sublime. A *Nature Trail* can be followed, and there are fine lake-shore walks at all times of year (see *Walk 6*, p.31).

The lake has a normal depth of 72ft, but during prolonged rain, when fed from the rapid water-courses from the high fells around, it can flood and spread up into Borrowdale and link up with Bassenthwaite Lake to the NW. After the Ice Age, in fact, both lakes were one, but silt has separated them.

The National Trust owns much of the lake and its shore. *St Herbert's Island* (also NT) is said to have held the hermitage of the Celtic saint (see *Keswick*). *Derwent Island*, to the N, has an odd history. In 1565 it was the home of a colony of German miners brought in during the great mining boom. In the 18th c. an eccentric, Joseph Pocklington, became the owner and built a mock fort, church, battery and Druid's circle: he also organised mock sea battles and regattas.

Derwent Water has always been a highway, and there is a regular boat service with 'request stops' at jetties. Boats can be hired at the Keswick boat landings. Trailed boats can be launched by arrangement with the Derwent Water Boat Club at *Portinscale*, or at *Nickol End Marine*, both at the NE end of the lake. Boats that can be manhandled may be launched at Kettlewell NT car park at the SE end of the lake.

The lake contains trout, perch and pike, and the vendace – a rare whitefish also found in Bassenthwaite.

See also *Borrowdale*.

Devoke Water
B3
Tarn 2m SE of Eskdale Green

Devoke Water compares in size with Rydal Water, but it is strictly a mountain tarn set in heathland. There is no road to the tarn, but it can be reached easily on foot along a bridleway from the Birker Fell road between *Eskdale Green* and *Ulpha*. The surrounding heathland is very rich in ancient settlements – Bronze Age and Iron Age – showing evidence of a surprisingly large population. Pollen analysis shows that ancient forests here gave way to cultivation. Later, climatic changes and heavy grazing reduced the productive soil to moorland.

Dove Cottage
C3(A)
Historic house ½m SE of Grasmere

Dove Cottage at Town End, Grasmere, receives many thousands of visitors from all over the world, for it is here that the genius of William Wordsworth was at its height. Here he wrote *The Prelude, Intimations of Immortality*, and very many of his shorter poems.

William and his sister Dorothy rented the house, which was formerly a tiny inn (*The Dove and Olive Branch*) in 1799. Dorothy fed him many ideas for his work. Her journal of that time, itself a work of considerable literary merit, gives a vivid account of their way of life there. In 1802 William married a childhood friend, Mary Hutchinson, and brought her to the cottage. A frequent visitor was his close friend Samuel Taylor Coleridge who lived for a time with his brother-in-law Robert Southey at Keswick. Among other celebrated visitors was Sir Walter Scott (as the Wordsworths were abstainers, he sought his dram at *The Swan Hotel*).

When the Wordsworths' fourth child was on the way in 1808 the cottage proved too small for the household, and they moved to Grasmere. The cottage was later tenanted by Thomas de Quincey who married a local girl, Peggy Simpson, and lived there for 22 years, filling the rooms with books.

The cottage, kept as it was in the Wordsworths' day, is open to the public. In a converted coach-house nearby is the splendid **Grasmere and Wordsworth Museum**, containing manuscripts, relics, displays, and a picture gallery.

Duddon Valley see *Dunnerdale*

Dunmail Raise B3
Road pass on A591, 2m N of Grasmere

Dunmail Raise is a pass between Grasmere and Thirlmere, walled in by the fells of Seat Sandal and Steel Fell. It is said to have been the scene of a battle in 945 between King Dunmail, a Norseman of Cumbria, and the Anglo-Saxon King Edmund of Northumbria. A large cairn between the dual carriageways marks the spot. It was once believed that Dunmail was buried here, but the historical evidence is that he lived on elsewhere. Another story tells how Dunmail fled eastwards over the pass by Grisedale Tarn, lightening his load on the way by casting his jewels and valuables into the water.

Dunmail is a natural boundary, and more than once has marked the border between England and Scotland. Until local government reorganisation in 1974, it marked the county boundary between Cumberland N and Westmorland S, and up to the last century, local people from either side of the Raise considered each other 'foreigners'. A local saying, on both sides, is 'Nowt good comes o'er t'Raise'.

Dunnerdale B3
Valley NW of Broughton-in-Furness

'The River Duddon' was the theme of a sonnet sequence by Wordsworth. Dunnerdale is the valley of the Duddon. Its attraction is in its great variety, with its falling waters, crags and woodlands. The crystal-clear Duddon rises at Wrynose Pass at the NW end of Coniston Old Man, which forms the great E rim of much of Dunnerdale. To the W are the fells of craggy Harter, and the heathlands of Birker, Ulpha and Thwaites. A narrow minor road runs down the valley. The head of Dunnerdale is covered with the conifer plantations of the Forestry Commission, which caused a great deal of controversy when planting began in 1936. The forest is accepted now, but a modest extension planned in 1983 opened old wounds.

At the N end of the forest is *Birks Bridge*, a lovely bridge spanning a narrow gorge with dark green pools below. To the S is the hamlet of **Seathwaite** (Norse, 'the clearing of the shieling'). Here lived the Rev Walker, the 'Wonderful Walker' mentioned by Wordsworth in *The Excursion*. Walker was the curate of Seathwaite for 66 years, living on a stipend of a few pounds a year. He and his wife spun, wove and made their own clothing. He worked as a farm labourer, taught the local children and served as doctor to the community. The couple raised a family and were generous to the poor, and yet when Walker died at the age of 92 he left £2000 in his will. He and his wife are buried in the churchyard and there is a commemorative plaque in the *Church*, which alas has been much altered.

The next hamlet is **Ulpha**, another Norse name. It has a small *Church*, handsomely poised on a little height (Wordsworth's 'Kirk of Ulpha'), and there is a row of *Almshouses*. Much of Ulpha's past had to do with mining and quarrying. At the bridge below Ulpha, the road divides. To the E of the river it goes to *Duddon Bridge* and to **Broughton-in-Furness*; to the W it is narrow and tortuous. At its foot, near Duddon Bridge, is the ruin of the 18th-c. *Duddon Forge*, managed by the National Park authority. Much of the building is remarkably intact. Ore was brought to the forge up the Duddon, charcoal was taken from the surrounding woodland, and the bellows were water-powered. The forge can be visited on application.

The Duddon once formed the boundary between Cumberland W and Lancashire E. It pours eventually onto *Duddon Sands*, once criss-crossed by highways, now abandoned to visiting wildfowl.

Easedale Tarn
B3(A)

Tarn NW of Grasmere

The Wordsworths called Easedale 'the black quarter', for it was from that direction that bad weather came to Grasmere. The tarn sits at 900ft and is a stirring sight after the steep pull up the public bridleway. It is a favourite walk from Grasmere, and it passes a skein of falling water known as '**Sour Milk Gill**'. A very wet route continues across Blea Rigg to Langdale.

Egremont
A3

Small town on A595, 6m S of Whitehaven. Event: Crab Fair (3rd Sat in Sep). EC Wed MD Fri. Inf (in season): Tel (0946) 820693

Like several other Cumbrian towns, Egremont has an impressively wide main street, where once there were open markets. The scale of the street gives the impression that a larger town extends beyond. The main attraction is the ruin of the Norman **Egremont Castle**. There are earthworks of an earlier structure, probably destroyed during the campaigns of David I of Scotland, but the present remains are of the stone castle built by William de Meschines in the 12th c. The castle subsequently passed through several families before it became ruinous in the 16th c. The curtain wall and gatehouse, with herringbone masonry, are 12th-c. work. Within the bailey are signs of a number of buildings. The hall to the N is thought to be 13th-c.

The legend of the horn which could be blown only by the true Lord of Egremont was told by Wordsworth. Hubert de Lucy, brother of the true Lord, Sir Eustace, villainously assumed possession of the castle when he thought that he had successfully organised the murder of his brother who was away on the Crusades. Sir Eustace returned when his brother was feasting, and blew the horn. Exit Hubert in haste by a side door!

The Egremont Crab Fair is said to date back continuously for seven centuries, when the then Lord of Egremont generously distributed crab apples to all. The apple cart still parades, and apples are thrown to the public. There are several amusing events including a pipe-smoking contest. But it is the 'gurning' competition which causes hilarity, when contestants try to pull the ugliest face, framed in a horse collar. Is this the origin of the term 'Crab-faced'?

Elter Water
B3(A)

Lake beside B5343, 4¼m W of Ambleside

Elter Water is the smallest of the lakes, and very irregular in shape. It sits at the foot of Langdale and takes water from the Langdale Beck; and the River Brathay flowing from Wrynose and down Little Langdale, after dropping down *Colwith Falls*, takes a northern twist to feed it. Its outflow is carried S by the much-augmented Brathay, which turns E at *Skelwith Force* to join the Rothay before entering Windermere.

The banks of Elter Water are reeded, and its only public access, a right of way on the E side of the lake, passes through alder woods. The best viewpoint is from the S approach on this path (see also Walk 3, p.31). The lake is in private ownership and the hamlet which takes its name from the lake, once noted for its gunpowder works, is now a holiday complex.

Ennerdale and Ennerdale Water
A2/B3

Dale and lake 8m NE of Egremont. Event: Ennerdale Show (last Wed in Aug)

Ennerdale is the most remote of the Lake District's dales, and its basin contains the waters of the River Liza and Ennerdale Water. Geologically the dale is interesting, and gives the landscape a great variety of forms. The mountains and peaks which tower at its head – Great Gable, Kirk Fell, Pillar, Steeple and Haycock – are typically of the Borrowdale Volcanic Series; the dale's middle reaches enter an exposure of granite, and the foot and the fells to the N penetrate the softer Skiddaw Slate Series. The latter accounts for the lake's 'banjo' shape, as the rocks at the foot yielded more easily to the grinding ice which carved out the dale in the Ice Age.

The head of the dale is blanketed in conifer forest. The planting was started in 1927 amid a growing controversy, which did much to promote the growth of concerned amenity societies. These societies and the National Park Authority proved their strength in the 1980s when the Water Authority, already impounding water from Ennerdale Water, proposed to enlarge the lake to provide water for the Nuclear Power industry. The plan was defeated after a public enquiry.

A sense of remoteness gives the dale and lake their appeal. The best viewpoint is **Bowness Knott** (NP), a hill to the E of the car park provided by the Forestry Commission. Here also are *Nature Trails* and a picnic site.

The lake contains trout and char, but its extreme clarity inhibits the presence of coarse fish. Boating is not allowed. At the end of August, the Ennerdale Show has hound-trailing, foxhound, terrier and sheepdog shows among other Cumbrian events.

Eskdale B3
Dale E of Ravenglass. Event: Eskdale Show (last Sat in Sep)

Eskdale is some 13½m long, and has everything that is best in Lake District landscape except a lake: broken cliffs of pink granite, walls of high fells, much broadleaved woodland, clear green river pools, waterfalls, and houses which seem to have grown from the ground. The dale's head is at *Esk Hause*, at 2490ft the Lake District's highest fell pass, a notorious spot for getting lost in bad weather. Here the River Esk starts before being heavily charged by waters from the towering fells: on its NE flank from Sca Fell and Scafell Pike, the highest land in England: and on its NE flank from Bow Fell's Lingcove Beck. The upper Esk is here unapproachable except to fell walkers, and the area could be classed as one of the wildest landscapes in England.

Hardknott Roman Fort overlooked the Britons' tracks coming down from the upper dale and from here, some-

where in the dale – no doubt part of it under the modern secondary road – is the Roman road to Ravenglass. In these remote mountains the Eskdale Show, in Autumn, shows classes of Cumbria's famous Herdwick sheep as well as holding fell racing, horn blowing and other traditional events. The Esk is fed again from Burnmoor by Whillan Beck, which flows past *Boot* to give power to its **Water Mill**, now restored by the County Council as a working museum. **St Catherine's Church** is down by the river. The setting is idyllic, but why here, away from the village? It is a typical small dale church, built like a barn, and largely 17th-c. The monks from Furness Abbey, which owned much of Eskdale, built a chapel here before this more recent church. Perhaps the site was originally occupied by a Celtic church, characteristically remote from centres of population.

Nearby is *Dalegarth*, the terminus of the **Ravenglass and Eskdale Railway**, a steam narrow-gauge which commutes through lovely woodland scenery between here and *Ravenglass*. The railway once transported ore from local iron mines and rock from the granite quarries; now it is run for visitors and dalesfolk. To the S of Dalegarth is **Stanley Gill Force** (NP), a waterfall in a beautifully wooded ravine laid out with paths and a viewpoint bridge (see *Walk 8*, p.32).

The dale's hamlet is *Eskdale Green*, the home of the Eskdale Outward Bound School. The dale, in utter contrast to its awesome start, ends green and mild under Muncaster Fell, with the Esk spilling into the sea at Ravenglass. The beautiful grounds of *Muncaster Castle* spread along the Esk Estuary.

Esthwaite Water B3(B)
Lake beside B5285, ½m S of Hawkshead

Wordsworth knew and loved Esthwaite well. When he was attending school at *Hawkshead* he would walk around the lake in 'that beloved vale', and he skated on the lake in winter. No towering fells about here, but green pasture, woods, and small settlements. The lake is 1½m long, and has three public access points: a strip of land owned by the Parish Council on the E side; a car park and access strip (NP) on the SW corner; and a public footpath from Hawkshead to the NW end. The lake is in private ownership. No power boats are allowed, and permits for rowing boats are obtainable from Hawkshead Post Office, or from Esthwaite How at Near Sawrey. The lake is rich in nutrient and contains perch, pike, rudd, roach and trout. At the lake head is a National Nature Reserve where the interest lies in the gradual transition from reeds, through fen, to woodland.

Fairfield C3
Fell N of Rydal

The Fairfield range is prominent in view from Windermere. In form it appears as a rough horseshoe, and the ridge round makes a popular whole-day walk. The ridge ends by *Rydal at Nab Scar and here it is notoriously steep, but has a good path. Continuing N there are two peaks, Heron Pike and Great Rigg Mann, before the summit of Fairfield is reached at 2863ft. Continuing along the E ridge, Hart Crag overlooks Deepdale towards Patterdale; further SE, Dove Crag overlooks Dovedale to the N; following S, High and Low Pikes are passed before the final descent. The S slopes, though craggy in places, are milder and greener than the N slopes, which are overhung with cliffs and ravines.

Far Sawrey see Sawrey

Furness Abbey B4
Abbey off A590, 1½m S of Dalton-in-Furness

The beautiful red sandstone ruins of Furness Abbey, crowded into 'the vale of the deadly nightshade', cannot fail to stir the imagination. Although they are outside the Lake District proper, they should not be overlooked. Immediately striking are the great W tower of the church and the chancel and transepts, standing almost to their former height.

Furness Abbey was originally in the charge of the monks of the Order of Savigny, who moved here from a site at Tulketh near Preston in 1127. 20 years later the Order was merged with the Cistercians, and ambitious building began. The land owned by the abbey included much of the Furness peninsula and part of Eskdale and Borrowdale: a vast area of woods, moors, peat bogs, pastures, rivers and lakes, copper, lead and iron mines. There were also growing possessions elsewhere, in places as far away as Ireland and the Isle of Man. So wealthy and powerful did the abbey become that when the Pope complained that an abbot had not made an obligatory journey to Rome, the recalcitrant remarked that if the Pope wished to see the Abbot of Furness he should come to Furness.

Of the church, the nave and transepts are 12th-c., the chancel 15th-c. Originally a belfry tower was attempted at the crossing, but it proved impracticable and instead the massive W tower was built (15th c.), extending partly into the W end of the nave. Both the window here, and the E window, were impressively large.

To the S of the church is the Cloister, with (E side) five beautiful moulded round-arched openings (13th-c). The second of these leads into the Chapter House (13th c.) with its window mouldings and parts of the piers supporting the vault surviving. The other openings off the E side of the cloister are: first and third, library rooms; fourth and fifth, entrances to dormitory undercroft and slype.

The remains of the Dormitory Undercroft, which originally had the dormitory above, show the latter to have been the largest in England (over 200ft long) and testify to the abbey's wealth and importance. The lay brothers were housed in the W Range, built in the 12th c. The S Range, containing the refectory, has now largely disappeared.

S of the main buildings was the Infirmary, which survives now in part of its hall and in its chapel and kitchen. The original infirmary stood to the E against the rock face, but this became the

Abbot's House. The *Guest House* is to the N. A wall once containing the 73-acre site of the abbey was plundered for building stone: after the Dissolution some of the stone was taken to repair the defensive tower at Dalton.

The abbey ruins are now cared for by the DoE. The public entrance leads through an interpretive display hall.

Glenridding C2
Village on A592, at SW end of Ullswater. Inf (in season): Tel (08532) 414

Glenridding's two claims to distinction are that it is the popular starting point for the ascent of the E side of *Helvellyn*, and for the Ullswater Navigation Company's 'steamer' service; the former from the S side of the bridge over Glenridding Beck, the latter from land projecting into Ullswater E of the village. This projecting land owes its existence to a mine disaster in 1927, when a dam providing a source of water power from high on Helvellyn burst open, bringing down hundreds of tons of debris into the lake.

Glenridding then was a prosperous mining town. The lead mines at Greenside above and to the W of the village were productive from the mid-17th c. until 1962, with the most profitable time in the 19th c. There is little left to see of the old workings, which are now in the ownership of the National Park Authority. Attempts are being made to establish trees and vegetation on the old tailing dams.

Glenridding today is a popular holiday village. A grave shortcoming is a shortage of public toilet facilities. Given the right winter conditions, Glenridding and Greenside are invaded by the hardy skiers who are prepared to tote their skis high up to the best snow slopes NE on *Raise*, an E appendage of Helvellyn.

Gosforth A3
Village off A595, 6½m SE of Egremont. Event: Gosforth Show (3rd Wed in Aug)

The notable feature of Gosforth is the unique, slender **Viking Cross** in *St Mary*'s churchyard. It is quite startling.

The carvings of the shaft (which, with the cross head, stands 14½ft), show both the Christian theme of good overcoming evil, and the Norse mythology. It dates from the 10th c. when the Vikings, having given up their habitual raiding, were coming across from Ireland and the Isle of Man, and settling extensively. In the church there are other Scandinavian or Saxon cross fragments, and two hogback tombs.

The Gosforth Show (August) has traditional exhibits of livestock and hound and terrier racing.

Grange-over-Sands C4
Small resort on Morecambe Bay on B5277, 13m SW of Kendal. EC Thur. Inf (in season): Tel (04484) 4026

The coming of the railway in 1857 made Grange-over-Sands ripe for development as a resort. But it never made the big-time, probably because the sands are estuary sands with a mud channel. This makes it an attraction for bird watchers, but impossible for bathers.

The railway is still here, and there is no better station at which to arrive: right alongside the promenade and open to the clean sea wind and the panorama of **Morecambe Bay**. *Kents Bank*, SW of the town, is the Furness end of the ancient public highway across the sands of the bay. This, too, is still there, and the guide who takes travellers through the channels and quicksands is still appointed by the Duchy of Lancaster and based at Kents Bank. Cross-bay walks are occasionally organised.

Although a holiday place, the town is spared vulgarity. The promenade is attractive; the row of Victorian shops with their cast-iron and glass shops is captivating, and the shops in the upper part of the town are pleasantly varied. Understandably it is a popular place for retirement, though the steep hills must cause problems for some.

The sands attract huge numbers of migratory birds, particularly knots and dunlins, for the winter climate is mild. There is a good walk up to *Hampsfell* (nature trail) NW of the town. The 'Hospice' on the top has a viewfinder.

Grasmere (Lake) (NT)   B3(A)
Lake beside A591, S of Grasmere village

This is, of course, Wordsworth's lake. Before later building he could see it from Dove Cottage, and it was the source of much inspiration. The lake is quite small, and only about 75ft deep. The best view is from *Loughrigg Terrace* (see *Walk 2*, p.31). The lake is owned by the National Trust; access to the shore is from *Dale End* southwards and from *Penny Rock Wood* (NP) on the SE. Light craft are allowed by permit on application to 'Padmire', Pavement End, Grasmere. There are boats for hire.

Grasmere (Village)   B3(A)
On B5287 (A591), 4m from Ambleside. Events: Rush-bearing (Sat nearest Aug 5), Grasmere Sports (3rd Thur after 1st Mon in Aug) EC Thur. Inf: Tel (09665) 245

'Not a single red tile, no gentleman's flaring house, or garden walls, break in upon the repose of this little, unsuspected paradise; but all is peace, rusticity, and happy poverty, in its neatest, most becoming attire'. So wrote Thomas Gray of Grasmere in 1769. This was more or less how Wordsworth found it, when he came to Dove Cottage 20 years later. No 'happy poverty' now, and at the height of the holiday season, little 'repose'. But there are still no red tiles and nothing glaringly commercial. Wordsworth is not exploited, and this is not another Stratford. The Wordsworths are buried under simple stones in the churchyard. St Oswald's Church is delightful, with varied architectural additions from the 13th c. The church had an earth floor until the last century, and it was customary to carpet it with rushes. Their annual replacement remains as a colourful ceremony with a procession of local children carrying flowers.

The Lake District's most popular sporting event takes place on the Grasmere Sports Field every August. A highlight is the 'Guides' Race', a gruelling ascent and leg-breaking descent of a steep-sided fell. Cumberland and Westmorland wrestling is also popular.

The village is a good walking centre.

Easy walks include circumnavigation of *Grasmere* and *Rydal Water* (see *Walks 1 & 2*, p.31), and ascents to *Easedale Tarn* and Alcock Tarn: Helvellyn and Fairfield, and the Langdale Fells, are also close by. *Dove Cottage*, Wordsworth's house, is at Town End ¼m SE. Between Grasmere and Rydal Water, a nature trail leads across *White Moss Common*.

Great Gable (NT)   B3
Fell NE of Wasdale Head. Event: Memorial Service on summit (Remembrance Sunday, nearest Sun to Nov 11)

From the head of *Wasdale*, it can be seen that Great Gable is well named. It seems to be the gable end of a monstrous house (2949ft high), and is one of the Lake District's challenges to fell walkers. The most popular ascent route is from the car park on *Honister Pass* to the N, which is cheating, as the pass summit reaches 1176ft. The ascent from Wasdale Head is either by *Sty Head*, or along a path up the Gable's W flank.

This, however, is also a rock climbers' fell. The climbing crags on the SE face are approached by the climbers' path, the *Girdle Traverse*, from Sty Head. Ascents include the famous *Napes Needle*, first climbed by the pioneer rock climber W.P. Haskett-Smith in 1886; he repeated the feat 50 years later, at the age of 74.

From Great Gable's rocky summit most of the Lake District's mountains can be seen, with the sea to the SW; a favourite view is from Sphinx Rock SW across Wasdale to Wast Water, walled in by the high fells.

Great Langdale   B3(A)
Dale on B5343, W of Ambleside

Great Langdale is alive with walkers and climbers all through the holiday season and every weekend through the winter, for here is everything they seek. The ring of high fells, *Langdale Pikes* (ranging N of the dale), *Pavey Ark, Bow Fell, Crinkle Crags* and *Pike of Blisco*, are the challenging valley walls; and beyond the W rim, *Scafell Pike* (3210ft) is within reach. Bow Fell

(2960ft) and Crinkle Crags (2816ft) stand highest in Langdale, and all but Pavey Ark top 2300ft. The rock climbs are mainly on the N side of the dale and on *Pavey Ark* and **Bow Fell*; beneath the NE fells, walkers can approach the 60ft **Dungeon Ghyll Force**, whose higher waters separate the Pikes.

Most of Langdale is in the care of the NT, including its farms and the large camp site, which is variegated and screened by trees, near the head of the valley at *Wall End*. From Wall End the road up the valley becomes narrow, steep and tortuous as it climbs S toward *Little Langdale* and passes *Blea Tarn*, a favourite viewpoint for the Langdale Pikes. *Chapel Stile*, the dale's settlement, stands by the road at the foot of the valley (E).

Great Salkeld see *Salkelds*

Grizedale Forest   B3(B)
Forest S and SW of Hawkshead & B5285

The Forestry Commission took over the Grizedale estate for afforestation in 1937. There had always been woodlands in the area. For several centuries, the woods were owned and managed by Furness Abbey. Now, large areas between **Esthwaite Water* and **Coniston Water* are covered in alien conifers; but credit must be given for the preservation of large areas of broadleaved trees, and for the fact that this was the first forest to open its gates for public recreation.

To the astonishment of many, the Hall was demolished after World War II. During the war it had housed German Officer POWs. The surviving outbuildings stand by the minor road to Satterthwaite, just over 3m from Hawkshead. One building, (**The Forest Visitor and Wildlife Centre**), now houses a Natural History Museum and a display showing the forest industry. There is also a restaurant, a hotel and Bill Grant's 'Theatre in the Forest', housed in a converted barn. A nature walk leads through *Millwood Forest*, and there is a waymarked walk along the 'Silurian Way'.

Hadrian's Wall   C1/D1
Ancient Monument 9m NE of Brampton

Hadrian's great Wall, started in 122AD and stretching from the Solway Firth to the Northumberland coast, is still seen extensively in the Northumberland National Park. By comparison, there is little left to see in Cumbria. The line has to be searched for. However, enthusiasts, after visiting the Roman section in Carlisle Museum, can follow a walkable section which leads W from *Gilsland*, by *Birdoswald*.

Planned as a 10ft wall behind a ditch, and defended by small forts at 1m intervals (milecastles), the W section was begun as a turf-work which was later largely replaced by stone. As the Barbarian opposition from N of the Wall proved more effective than expected, larger forts were built astride it; at *Birdoswald* a 5-acre fort is just visible above the River Irthing, and the Wall itself survives there, with gates and even wheel-ruts.

To protect the vulnerable coastal reaches of the system, the Romans extended its defences S along the Cumbrian coast. The threat from within the Lake District was contained by the forts which can still be seen at **Ravenglass*, **Ambleside* and **Brougham*.

Hardknott Pass   B3
Pass 13m W of Ambleside

Hardknott is on the route from Ambleside via Little Langdale and Wrynose Pass to Eskdale. The winding narrow road, with sections 1:3 and with hairpin bends, rises to 1291ft. It is the most testing road in England. Many motorists seek out the test; most others find themselves there by accident, having seen from the road map that the route appears to be the most direct E to W across the central fells. The weekend snarl-up is normal as stalled vehicles block the road, vehicles meet at narrow sections with no room to pass, or passengers have to get out and push. What would the Romans – who improved the original road and built a fort (SW) to guard it – make of this confusion?

Hardknott Roman Fort B3

Ancient monument on Hardknott Pass, 13m W of Ambleside, 6½m E of Eskdale Green

When Agricola became Roman Consul of Britain in 78AD, his engineers not only made new roads, but 'improved' the British ones. One such improved road, actually chiselled through bedrock in places, was the route over *Wrynose* and *Hardknott* Passes. During the reign of Hadrian, (117-138AD), a cohort of auxiliaries who had marched all the way from Dalmatia (modern Yugoslavia) came over the passes to build a stone fort on an 800ft plateau overlooking Eskdale. They called it Mediobogdum, 'the fort in the middle of the bend'.

No Roman fort in the country has a more startling and dramatic site. Seen from the fell above, its ruins seem poised on a ledge like an eagle's eyrie. The walls are now preserved by the DoE. Originally they stood 12ft high. Some of the stone used was dressed sandstone, transported some 20m from the W coast. The inscription over the gate, dedicating the fort to Hadrian and identifying the builders, was on a slate slab presumably brought from Langdale (the surviving fragments are in Carlisle Museum). The fort is built in the standard 'playing-card' design covering 3 acres, with doors in each wall, even though the one on the W opens onto a cliff edge (the rubbish exit?). Below the fort is the bathhouse with the round *laconicum*, the 'hot-dry room'.

Another startling feature is above the fort to the NE. In an area covered with stones and devoid of even ground, a large *parade-ground* for drilling (and sports?) has been cleared and levelled. The foundations of the Commander's house, HQ building and granaries can be seen within the fort. The rest of the buildings, housing 500 men, would have been of wood.

Why was the fort here? It could be presumed that it overlooked the traffic on busy British roads. The Roman road it protected, too, was a link between the important Roman port and fort at *Ravenglass*, and the fort at *Ambleside*. Although the two latter forts were in use until the late 4th c., it is thought that Mediobogdum was abandoned for some reason two centuries earlier.

Haweswater C2/C3

Lake 5m W of Shap

Once there was a village of Mardale in a green valley with dairy farms around the lake of Haweswater. In 1929 Manchester Corporation had acquired all the valley, and started building a dam. Eventually, village and farms were submerged as the water rose by 95ft. The church and the inn were lost. The Corporation fulfilled the corporal need and built *The Haweswater Hotel*, which would have looked very fine in Manchester. Now all the controversy is past, and Haweswater is accepted as a quiet place to visit and to walk around. The Water Authority no longer discourages public access to the gathering area.

Hawkshead B3(A)

Village on B5285 (B5286), 5m SW of Ambleside. Event: Hawkshead Show (1st Tue in Sep). EC Thur (winter). Inf (in season): Tel (09666) 525

Hawkshead was an important wool market in Norman times, controlled by Furness Abbey which owned much land in the area, and by the Manor of which only the 15th-c. *Gatehouse* and one wing (now a farmhouse) remain. The town suffered indirectly but badly from the Dissolution, but a market continued to serve the area until Ulverston established itself as a thriving port, and sapped Hawkshead's trade.

Wordsworth was a pupil at the little **Grammar School** by the church, and to visit it is to step back in time. The poet's desk, with his name carved on it by his own hand, is still there. William lodged in a cottage here for a while with Ann Tyson, 'Kind and motherly dame', and when she moved to nearby Colthouse, he moved with her.

Today, Hawkshead is a village of very attractive timber-framed buildings, arches, and yards. **St Michael's Church** dates from the 15th c., but has

69

earlier foundations. There are some captivating decorations and painted texts of the 17th c. On the N side of the village is the 15th-c. **Old Courthouse** (NT).

The car park is too large for the village, and some modern shops designed to attract tourists rather spoil the village's essential character. An out-of-season visit is more rewarding. 3m NW is the well known beauty spot, *Tarn Hows*, and Hawkshead makes a good starting point for walks to and around the tarn (see *Walk 9*, p.32).

The Hawkshead Show (September) exhibits livestock, including Herdwick sheep. Hound trailing and horse jumping are among other competitive events.

Helm Crag
B3(A)
Fell NW of Grasmere

Helm Crag is an essential feature in the Grasmere scene. It is of modest height (1299ft), but it has a very rugged top. A rock formation seen from Grasmere suggests a lion with a lamb between its front feet, hence the fell's other name 'The Lion and the Lamb'. Another rock seen from the W of the fell suggests a person seated at an organ. From the NE by Dunmail, another suggests a howitzer. The ascent from *Grasmere* is rather steep and nasty, but the views are worth the effort.

Helvellyn
B2
Fell E of Thirlmere

Helvellyn attracts more fell walkers than any other mountain in England. It is easily accessible, and perhaps its Celtic name adds to the attraction. The summit is at 3116ft, but there are interesting subsidiary summits along the 6m ridge, all rising higher than 2750ft. *Dollywaggon Pike* is its S bastion. To the N is *Nethermost Pike*, and N of the highest point are *Lower Man*, *Raise*, *Stybarrow Dod* and *Great Dod*.

Generous time allowances are necessary for ascents. The starting points from the W are from *Grasmere via Grisedale Tarn*, a long walk; from *Wythburn by Thirlmere*, short but very steep; from *Thirlmere via Helvellyn Gill*,

a good route. The E ascents are more exciting. The most popular route of all is from *Glenridding by Striding Edge*, a narrow arête with an uncomfortable scramble finish; or by *Swirral Edge*. The latter routes can be insidiously dangerous in cold weather, as they quickly ice up. Indeed, in all seasons but high summer the mountain needs to be treated with great care, and in snow conditions it is for experienced fell walkers only. Snow stays longer on the N side of Raise, which is where the skiers make for, but it is a long haul, carrying gear, from the nearest access point at Greenside W of Glenridding.

High Street
C3
Fell W of Haweswater

High Street is an unlikely name for a high fell, but in fact this long N-S ridge was the route of a Roman road along an improved British road. The high way was chosen to avoid forests and swamps at lower levels. The 8m-long ridge proper starts from the S at *Garburn Pass*, a track linking the long valleys of Troutbeck and Kentmere, and the main peaks are all over 2300ft: *Yoke*, *Ill Bell*, *Froswick*, *Thornthwaite Crag*, High Street *summit* (2663ft), and *High Raise*. The plateau is green, and for years it was the scene of annual shepherds' meets when stray sheep were exchanged and festivities enjoyed, including a horse race held just by the summit on what is still known as '*Racecourse Hill*'.

Holker Hall
B4
Historic house off B5278, 5m W of Grange-over-Sands. Event: Rose Show (2nd weekend in Jul)

A splendid Victorian building, replacing a previous house gutted by fire in 1871. It is in the Elizabethan style, in red sandstone. A wing remains of the 17th-c. house, which was built for the Preston family (Richard Preston was the Prior at Cartmel at the Dissolution). By marriage the property passed through the Lowther family to the present owners, the Cavendish family.

The house is open to the public, and has a pleasant 'lived in' atmosphere, with a minimum of barriers. The rooms are delightful, with fine decor, pictures and *objets d'art*. Historic items include a face-screen worked by Mary Queen of Scots. Of special note are the carved staircase and dining-room fireplace, made by local craftsmen.

Stretching towards Morecambe Bay, the *Grounds* are worth a visit in their own right. Joseph Paxton, designer of the Crystal Palace, had a hand here. He planted the Chile Pine ('monkey puzzle tree') which is now massive. It was once blown down in a gale, pulled upright again by seven cart-horses, and pinned down. In the outbuildings are the **Lakeland Motor Museum** and the *Lakeland Craft Centre*, well designed and interesting. The *Deer Park* has one of England's oldest herds of fallow deer. Many events are organised in the grounds, including the Lakeland Rose Show, and regular hot-air balloon ascents.

*Cartmel Priory is 2½m NW.

Honister Pass (NT) B2
On B5289, 8½m SW of Keswick

The Borrowdale road from Keswick leaves the head of the dale near Seatoller, and continues to Buttermere over this 1190ft pass. The descent to *Buttermere is very steep. To the S of the pass summit are massive quarry-workings. The slate, composed of sedimentary volcanic dust and ash, is very hard, and is valued as building stone. High-quality roofing slate has long been one of the quarry's products. A car park has been sited below the quarry, and is popular with fell walkers, as it is the best starting point for the easiest route to *Great Gable (2949ft) to the S – at the heart of some of the highest, wildest and least accessible country in the Lake District. A path N leads to *Dale Head* (2743ft). (See also *Walk 4*, p.31.)

Hutton-in-the-Forest C2
Historic house on B5305 6m NW of Penrith (Exit 41, M6)

A 14th-c. pele tower is the nucleus of this odd mixture of buildings. Later additions are the 17th-c. N wing and Baroque front, and the 19th-c. medieval-style tower which rises above the house. Inside, the 17th-c. staircase survives and the collection of pictures, tapestries and furniture covers four centuries. The formal gardens and terraces were laid out in the 17th c., and there is a delightful woodland walk.

Irton Cross A3
Historic monument off A595, 3m SE of Gosforth

In the churchyard of *St Paul's*, with its views of mountains and coast, is a remarkably well preserved 9th-c. cross. 10ft high, it is elaborately carved with geometric designs on its shaft, and has retained its head. The presence here of an Anglian cross so near the Viking cross at *Gosforth might suggest a peaceful co-existence between the two races.

Kendal C3
Pop 21,600. 22m N of Lancaster (A6/M6). Events: Kendal Gathering, Kendal Jazz Festival, Kendal Folk Festival, Westmorland County Show (dates variable, but usually late Aug-early Sep). EC Thur MD Wed, Sat. Inf: Tel (0539) 25758

'Wool is my Bread' is the motto of the ancient, hard-working town of Kendal. Now its diet is more varied, but it remains busy. The grey stone town on the River Kent, with some of its timber-frame buildings surviving, is a place of character, despite misguided attempts at modernisation. Kendal's ever-present curse is a one-way system which, in spite of a by-pass, funnels fast and noisy traffic down the length of the main streets. It is a serious hazard and annoyance to pedestrians.

The first known settlement was S of the present town, at Watercrook. The Romans built a fort, Alauna, following Agricola's northern campaign in 79AD. A settlement grew around the fort, and presumably survived with varying fortunes for three centuries. By the time of the Norman Conquest, the town had moved N to its present position. A castle, now called Castle Howe, was built on a commanding prospect W of the town centre. It may have been of timber; only the earthworks remain. The town suffered from the border conflicts and raids, especially that carried out by the Earl of Fife in 1210. Some time before this, a more substantial stone castle was built E of the river on what is now called Castle Hill. This withstood the raids, and in the 16th c. it was the home of Katherine Parr, widow of Henry VIII. The castle became a ruin in the 16th c.

Kendal's wealth came from the wool · trade, which flourished from the 14th c. 'Kendal Green', a heavy cloth, became famous (it was mentioned by Shakespeare in *Henry IV*), and Kendal's knitted stockings were much sought-after. Later the leather and tobacco trades flourished; the tobacco was imported via the busy W-coast port of Whitehaven. The trades survive in the shoe factories S of the town, and the snuff factory. One modern industry is the manufacture of Kendal Mint Cake, a delicious and energy-giving confection used by fell-walkers and climbers.

Construction of the impressive **Church of the Holy Trinity** probably began early in the 12th c. The church is at the S end of the town by the river, and its size is immediately striking, reflecting the prosperity of the wool merchants who endowed it. It is the second widest parish church in England (103ft), only 3ft narrower than York Minster. The nave and two inner aisles, and the W wall, are thought to originate from the 12th c. The *SE Chapel* was added by the Parr family in the early 14th c., and to the W of this the *Flemish Aisle* (named from imported Flemish weavers who helped found the town's prosperity) was added. The *N aisle* and the *Lady Chapel* were added in the 16th c. by Sir Roger Bellingham, and a fine brass effigy (1533) shows Sir Roger and his wife. A helmet and sword are displayed on the N wall. The helmet may have belonged to Sir Roger, but there is a story that it belonged to 'Robin the Devil' (see *Belle Isle).

The church was once covered with paintings and decoration. In the 17th c. it is recorded that the interior was painted with serpents and dragons, cherubims and seraphims, and texts.

The exterior had yellow and black margins around doors and windows.

Just N of the church is a fine 18th-c. house, **Abbot Hall**, now an art gallery housing frequent exhibitions as well as a permanent collection of Georgian silver, porcelain, furniture and paintings. In the hall's stable block is the very splendid **Museum of Lakeland Life and Industry**, the best museum in the county. It contains exhibits of local industry, including hill farming, and imaginative displays capturing the flavour of social life in the Lake District's past. (Across the river, in Aynam Road, is the *Goodacre Carpet Factory* which offers guided tours.)

Returning to the church and proceeding N up Kirkland into Highgate, the 18th-c. *Brewery House* is on the left. The old brewery behind is now the town's arts centre. Further on opposite *The New Inn*, on the right, is Yard 83. This is *Dr Manning's Yard* and is worthy of inspection, for the whole town was originally built around a system of yards such as this, with narrow entries to the main street. It used to be thought that the system was created as a defence against raids, but it is more likely that the yard was adopted as a handy working area with the workers housed around it, and the entries closeable for privacy and security. Once Kendal had 150 yards of varying size and shape, but they have been fast disappearing under redevelopment schemes.

Further on is the *Town Hall* (1893), which houses the information centre and a special treasure: the prayer-book of Katherine Parr. In front of it stands the *Calling Stone*, once probably the base of a town cross, and traditionally used for proclamations. Across the road is All Hallows Lane. This is probably the best place for listening to the Town Hall's carillon (if traffic noise permits), which is played every three hours from 9 am to 9 pm, with a different tune for each day of the week. The lane climbs steeply and continues left into Beast Banks. A little way up here a narrow walkway, Garth Heads, leads left to a good view over the town. From here

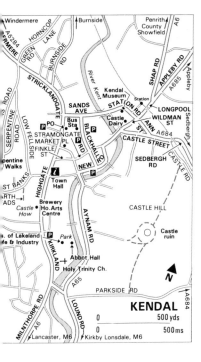

offal, the shops were moved to the New Shambles in the 19th c.

Below Old Shambles at the beginning of the town's main street, Stricklandgate, is the timber-framed *Old Fleece Inn*, dating from 1654. Opposite, and a little left, is the Market Place. Some way along on the right from the Market Place is an entry into the *New Shambles*, now containing some attractive shops. This was built on a slope, the better to remove the flow of butchers' refuse and deposit it into the river. The Shambles emerges into Finkle Street. Going left, one can see another fragment of old cobbled Kendal, *Branthwaite Brow*. Continuing through, Stramongate leads to a bridge. Across the bridge is Wildman Street, and here the town's oldest stone building, *The Castle Dairy*, is in use as it was in Katherine Parr's day. It is now a restaurant, but opens in season on Wednesday afternoons for public inspection. Around the next corner (Station Road) is Kendal's **Museum of Natural History and Archaeology**, with well arranged displays worthy of a leisurely visit.

The **castle ruin** is reached by taking Ann Street opposite Station Road, turning left up Castle Street, then right along Castle Road, and turning right again shortly afterwards. Much time can be spent in exploration around the old buildings, the lanes and yards of Kendal; there are also riverside walks, and above the town on the W side the *Serpentine Walks* lead through attractive woodland.

Kentmere C3
Dale off A591, NW of Kendal

The River Kent rises under High Street fells and flows down Kentmere before reaching Kendal and Levens Bridge. Kentmere lacks its lake. The shallow, reedy remnant of a lake was drained in the 19th c., to 'improve' agricultural land. A tarn at the dale head has been impounded by a dam. The minor road peters out at the hamlet; the road W over *Garburn Pass* is ruinous and eroded, offering only a good walkers'

there is a climb up to **Castle Howe**, across the earthworks of Kendal's original castle. The motte and bailey are still discernible. At the top of the hill is an obelisk, erected in 1788, commemorating the 1688 'revolution' – the arrival of William of Orange on the abdication of James II.

Returning via Beast Banks to All Hallows Lane, a diversion can be made left down Low Fellside and then left again to another part of old Kendal, *Sepulchre Lane*. It is cobbled, and there are intriguing glimpses of old lanes all round. From a viewpoint up this lane, it is possible to see over the town and to make out the old yard structures. Back on Low Fellside, below All Hallows Church, an old gateway on the left leads down steps to the *Old Shambles*. Here, in old times, were the town's butchers' shops; but because the drainage could not satisfactorily remove the blood and route with access to the S end of the *High Street* range. The head of the valley is also the preserve of walkers looking for somewhere quieter than the popular tourist routes. Harter Fell (2539ft), at the head, is a splendid peak. *Nan Bield Pass*, also at the head, is the walkers' route to *Haweswater*, and offers some of the Lake District's wildest scenery.

Keswick
B2

Town on A66, 16m W of Penrith. Event: Keswick Show (late Summer Bank Hol Mon). EC Wed (winter) MD Sat. Inf: Tel (0596) 72645

An early guide book states: 'The full perfection of Keswick consists of three circumstances: beauty, horror and immensity united'. The beauty is certainly still there unspoiled. Friar's Crag, in spite of its obvious popularity, is still one of the best viewpoints in the Lake District, with Derwent Water before and Keswick vale all round, and the magnificent backcloth of Skiddaw. 'Horror', in the Georgian sense, was suggested by the perilous-looking crags: nowadays, some would say that Keswick's real horror is a bank holiday with crowded car parks, shops and public houses. But although Keswick is one of the top three holiday resorts in the Lake District and the rock-climbers' base, it is not always so crowded.

The stone-built town itself has character, and commands its devotees. In the 16th and 17th c. Keswick was an important mining town; copper ore came by lake and road from the many mines in the area. In 1565 German mining experts were settled, some marrying local girls. The woods were devastated to make charcoal, and the town was under a constant pall of smoke from the many furnaces, their bellows powered by water wheels. 'Wad', or black lead, was found in Borrowdale, and laid the foundation of the pencil-making industry. A busy factory survives, although the 'lead' is now made from imported material.

The eventual decline of the mines coincided with Keswick's rise as a tourist centre. The poet Robert Southey made his home here in 1803, sharing his house for a time with the Coleridge family: the Wordsworths were frequent visitors. But the real impact on Keswick was the coming of the railway from Penrith in 1864, the date of many of the buildings in the town. Alas, the line is now axed, and replaced by the A66.

In the town centre is the *Moot Hall* (Town Hall), an attractive building standing on an island site. It dates from 1813, and replaced an earlier building. It now houses the *Tourist Information Centre*, jointly run by the National Park and the tourist authorities. At the NW end of the main street, by the River Greta, is the **Cumberland Pencil Mill**. A fascinating little museum here tells the story of pencil making (the world's first pencils were made in Keswick), and the old machines and early pencils are on display. On the left by Greta Bridge is the *Old Mill*, now a Youth Centre, a relic of Keswick's wool-producing days. On the opposite side of the river are the workshops of *Keswick Industrial Arts*, founded by Canon H.D. Rawnsley, one of the founders of the National Trust.

The oldest building is **St Kentigern's Church**, further NW at *Crosthwaite*, ¾m from the town centre. This is thought to have been the site of a cross erected to mark the visit of the Celtic saint (otherwise known as St Mungo, the patron saint of Glasgow). This was probably followed by a wooden chapel before the building of the Norman church. Foundations of this building (12th-c.) survive in the N aisle wall of the present church, and the chapel dates from the 14th c. Other features, particularly windows, show further building into the 16th c. The church was completely restored by Sir George Gilbert Scott in 1844. Monuments include a 15th-c. effigy of a man and wife, and a marble figure of Robert Southey, the Poet Laureate, with an epitaph composed by his friend William Wordsworth, who succeeded him as Laureate. Southey's grave is in the churchyard. Canon Rawnsley was vicar of Crosthwaite for 34 years in the last century.

Keswick's parish church, *St John the Evangelist*, is S of the Moot Hall in the town centre. Designed by Anthony Salvin in 1838, it is a fine sandstone building with a spire. In the SW corner of the churchyard is the grave of the novelist Sir Hugh Walpole (d.1941).

Keswick's museum, the **Fitz Park Museum and Art Gallery**, stands near the park in Station Road. It has a varied collection: manuscripts by Southey, Wordsworth, Coleridge and Walpole; geology and natural history specimens. A novelty is the unique instrument with tuned musical stones, once played by royal command at Buckingham Palace for Queen Victoria. The stones were collected locally.

Another museum worth visiting is the *Keswick Railway Museum*, in the redundant railway station.

Keswick's big attraction is, of course, the lake shore with the boat landings. A regular boat service circles *★Derwent Water* in both directions, offering opportunities for shore walks around the lake (see *Walks 6 & 7*, ps. 31 & 32). Beyond the boat landings is **Friar's Crag** (NT), a promontory easily reached even by wheel-chair. This is the great viewpoint up-lake into the magnificent Jaws of Borrowdale. Here, tradition has it, the visiting friars would stand to await blessing from St Herbert who occupied a hermitage on what is now called St Herbert's Isle. St Herbert was a great friend of St Cuthbert of Holy Island, off the coast of Northumbria. Just by Friar's Crag is a memorial stone to John Ruskin, quoting his remark that a visit to the viewpoint was one of his earliest memories. By the Lakeside Car Park, N of Friar's Crag, is the *Century Theatre*, which has a professional repertory in season.

There are many walks in the area. For the energetic there is the ascent of *★Skiddaw* (3053ft), one of the four highest mountains in England. In fine weather this offers no problems, as the routes are quite clear and there is no rough scrambling, but it should be regarded as a whole-day expedition. The ascent of **Latrigg**, the fell lying close to the town, offers a shorter walk, with fine views over Keswick and Derwent Water (see *Walk 5*, p.31). Shorter still, but a 'must', is the mild ascent of **Castle Head** (529ft), SE of the town and an easy walk. The rocky hill is thought to be an ancient volcanic 'plug': the views are excellent. There are also the lake-shore walks, and many good walking routes S in Borrowdale.

For two weeks in July, Keswick becomes the focal point of the Christian Convention, and many committed Christians from all over Britain and abroad occupy the town and the temporary camping fields. During the bank holiday in late August, the Keswick Show exhibits livestock and stages hound-trailing as well as Cumberland and Westmorland wrestling.

On the E outskirts of the town

KESWICK

By-Pass, Bothel, A66 / Latrigg, Skiddaw

Cumberland Pencil Mill (Mus.)

Keswick Industrial Arts Workshop

Old Mill

MAIN STREET

River Greta

Fitz Park

Keswick Railway Museum

Fitz Park Mus. & Art Gallery

Old Windebrowe

TITHEBARN ST.

BANK

ST PO

VICTORIA ST.

THE HEADLANDS

HEADS ROAD

Moot Hall

A591 PENRITH ROAD

Penrith, A66 Windermere, A591

MARKET RD.

ST JOHN

ST

LAKE / BORROWDALE

ROAD

THE HEADS

row Park

LAKE ROAD

St John the Evangelist

AMBLESIDE ROAD

Century Theatre

went

er

CASTLE HEAD (529')

N

iars Crag   Borrowdale

B5289

0   500 yds

0   500 ms

(Penrith road) is **Old Windebrowe** (open summer only) which was once lived in by Wordsworth and his sister Dorothy (1794), and has rooms preserved in the style and furnishings of the period.

S of Portinscale off the A66, 1m W of Keswick, are the gardens of **Lingholm**. Overlooking Derwent Water, with splendid views of Borrowdale, these extensive woodland gardens planted with rhododendrons, azaleas and other shrubs offer a 1½m garden walk.

Kirkby Lonsdale D4
Village off A65 (M6/A683), 12m SE of Kendal. EC Wed MD Thur. Inf: Tel (0468) 71603

Kirkby Lonsdale is a pleasant village with some fine old houses and streets. The views over the **River Lune** are notable. Ruskin enthused about them; Turner painted a scene from the churchyard. The village is very busy on market days, and car parking can be a problem.

The Norman Church, **St Mary's**, near Market Street, is one of the best in the district. The heavy columns and arches of the N side of the nave are early 12th-c. With their diamond patterning, reminiscent of Durham Cathedral, they present a mystery, for they are quite out of scale with the other more modest proportions of the interior.

The main street ends at the medieval *'Devil's Bridge'*, now traffic-free. The rocks and water beneath provide an informal pleasure ground in the summer.

Kirkby Stephen D3
Village on A685, 24m NE of Kendal. EC Thur MD Mon. Inf: Tel (0930) 71804

A friendly little market village and a good touring centre for off-the-beaten-track *Eden Valley*. Good walks in the immediate area. The fine church, **St Stephen's**, represents many building periods since the 13th c. There is an interesting fragment of a 10th-c. *cross* with the 'Bound Devil'; or is it Loki, the Viking equivalent? In the N chapel is the 16th-c. effigy of Lord Wharton, the ruthless scourge of the Scots in the border troubles. In the S chapel is a 15th-c. effigy, possibly of Sir Richard

de Musgrave, who was no friend of the Scots either, or of nature conservationists: he is said to have killed the last wild boar.

4m S of the village on Mallerstang Common, overlooking the Eden Valley, stands the ruin of *Pendragon Castle*. The original late-Norman pele tower was restored by Lady Anne Clifford in 1660, but little now remains; the crumbling walls survive as a rare example of this region's medieval fortress towers still standing independent of any extension or addition. The ruin, with its dramatic setting, is associated with King Arthur, whose father Uther Pendragon is said to have built a castle here. Permission to visit must be obtained from the landowner.

Kirkoswald C1
Village on B6412, 11m NE of Penrith

Once an important market town, Kirkoswald is now a very attractive little village. **St Oswald's Church** is unusual, being completely detached from its 18th-c. bell tower. It was no doubt thought that the latter would be more audible and conspicuous on the hill above the medieval church, which sits in a hollow. The church stands here as a result of the ancient policy to site Christian churches on pagan religious sites. There was a magic well here, whose outflow comes under the W wall. There are signs that there was an earlier wooden church, but the present stone structure is 12th-c. with 14th, 15th and 16th-c. alterations. The ancient wooden porch is remarkable. The church is connected to the very fine 17th-c. *College* by an avenue of limes.

To the SE, the 13th-c. Norman **Castle** of Ralph Engayne is a sketchy ruin. 1½m to the NW of the village is the *Nunnery*, built in 1715 over the foundations of a 12th-c. Benedictine house. For a small charge there is access to the grounds beside the River Eden and to the **Nunnery Walks**, a choice of several very pleasant routes (slippery in wet weather) through woodland, by cascades, and along riverside paths carved into sandstone cliffs.

Kirkstone Pass C3
On A592, 7m N of Windermere

The pass takes its name from a large boulder near the summit which in fog or fading light could be mistaken for a dale church. At 1450ft this is the highest road pass in the Lake District, and *The Kirkstone Pass Inn* can claim to be the highest hostelry. The route S for *Windermere* overlooks the green valley of *Troutbeck*, and the route N for *Patterdale* enjoys a view over Brothers Water. The minor road which also reaches the pass summit from *Ambleside* is, in its last section, called 'The Struggle' – a particularly apt name, one would imagine, in the age of the coach and horse, when passengers had to walk. There are extensive quarry operations to the SW.

Lanercost Priory C1
Priory ruin off A69, 2½m NE of Brampton

The priory, situated by the River Irthing, was founded by Robert de Vaux in 1166 as an Augustinian house. So near the border, it was misused by both Scots and English: Edward I used it as a campaign base on three occasions. The final blow of the Dissolution also put an end to the monks, who were executed for their part in the Pilgrimage of Grace. The N aisle of the priory *Church* was rescued for use as a parish church, and the picturesque ruins of the priory itself include part of the tower, choir, clerestory and undercroft. The best preserved walls, on the W range, are those of Sir Thomas Dacre's house, built for him within the priory after the Dissolution: a pele tower, once the prior's quarters, is incorporated to the S.

Levens Hall C3
Historic house on A6 (A590) 5m S of Kendal

Like many other old houses in the area Levens Hall was built as an extension to a 14th-c. pele tower. The tower was sold to Alan Bellingham in the 16th c. and under his descendants the mansion took shape (1580-90). In 1688 the house passed to Colonel James Graham who employed a Monsieur Beaumont to design his garden: the result, faithful to the original design, is the haunting topiary we see today.

The lofty, oddly-shaped house is built of rough stone: the pele tower still stands to the right of the entrance. Inside there is fine plasterwork and panelling, particularly in the *Great Hall*, two *Drawing Rooms* and *Dining Room*. The rooms also have superb carved chimneypieces. Much of the furniture is *c*. 1700 and there are many documents of historical interest. The house is now owned by the Bagot family, and open to the public in the summer. A collection of steam engines and models is housed in an outbuilding.

Sizergh Castle (NT) is 3m N.

Little Langdale B3(A)
Dale off A593, W of Ambleside

Little Langdale is S of Great Langdale and separated from it by Lingmoor Fell and Blake Rigg. A narrow road passing fine views of **Blea Tarn** (NT) connects them. At the head of the dale is *Wrynose Pass*, and from here the Roman road from Hardknott follows the source of the River Brathay which runs through the pretty *Little Langdale Tarn* and eventually into Windermere. Wetherlam, a bulky spur of the Coniston Old Man range, makes the S wall of the dale. Mines and quarries were for long a major source of wealth for the dale.

Little Salkeld see *Salkelds*

Lodore Falls see *Borrowdale*

Long Meg and Her Daughters C2
Stone circle off A686, 8m NE of Penrith

'A weight of awe, not easy to be borne,
Fell suddenly upon my Spirit – cast
From the dread bosom of the unknown past,
When first I saw that sisterhood forlorn.'

So wrote Wordsworth when he came upon this Bronze Age stone circle, one of the most important archaeological sites in Britain. The circle of 59 stones, the 'daughters', is over 100yds in diameter, while 'Long Meg', a 12ft megalith like a pointing finger, stands 70ft away. Long Meg bears the mysterious 'cup and ring' carving commonly seen elsewhere on northern standing stones. There is evidence of dressing in some of the stones, and the shapes generally suggest the pattern of the great circle of Avebury in Wiltshire. The alignment of the stones is thought to be with the mid-winter sun.

About ½m NE lies another circle, *Little Meg*, with 11 stones.

Longsleddale C3
Dale off A6, N of Kendal

A narrow road by the River Sprint once connected Kendal with Mardale; but Mardale was drowned when Hawes-water's level was raised by Manchester Corporation's reservoir works. So now Longsleddale, the route of the road, remains a quiet seldom-visited cul-de-sac, and *Gatescarth Pass* to Haweswater is a walkers' route. The lake is accessible by car only from the NE. A path from the top of Gatescarth is the best ascent point for *Harter Fell* (2539ft) whose summit, with nearby farmland, is in care of the National Trust.

Loughrigg B3(A)
Fell W of Ambleside

Loughrigg Fell is close to Ambleside, and is deservedly very popular. On the N side is *Loughrigg Terrace*, an easily approached, broad, level track giving classic views over *Grasmere* (see *Walk 2*, p.31). The summit of the fell has many small peaks. A favourite prospect is S over the head of Windermere from *Todd Crag*. The true summit, 1099ft, is at the fell's W end. *Loughrigg Tarn* is to the SW, and the view across it to Langdale Pikes is a favourite of photographers (see also *Walk 3*, p.31). E of Loughrigg, just N of Ambleside, is the starting point for a *Nature Trail* across the fell.

Loweswater (NT) A2
Lake off B5292, 8m S of Cockermouth. Event: Loweswater Show (3rd Thur in Sep)

Loweswater is only 1m long, but it has a beautiful setting and cannot be ignored. It is unique because its waters flow inwards towards the centre of the Lake District, whereas all the other

lakes flow outwards into radiating watercourses. Loweswater's outflow runs across a flat plain, where the village stands, into *Crummock Water*. It contains pike, perch and trout. The lake and its wooded shores are cared for by the National Trust; a footpath runs through *Holme Wood* (NT) on the SW shore, and boats can be hired. Private launching is not permitted on this small lake.

The Loweswater Agricultural Show in the early autumn has traditional regional attractions.

Lowther Park C2
Parkland off A6 (M6), 4½m S of Penrith. Event: Lowther Horse Driving Trials & Country Fair (early Aug)

The Lowther Estate has been owned by the Lowther family since the 13th c. The Hall was lost in a fire in the 18th c., and a very extravagant new Hall was built by the 5th Earl of Lonsdale in 1806. In 1936, as maintenance proved too costly, it was demolished, leaving only its spectacular *façade*: a monument to the industry of Sir Robert Smirke, whose local reputation was founded on this, his first commission (undertaken when he was 25). *St Michael's Church* to the N is medieval, with 17th-c. exterior restoration by Sir John Lowther, who also built the first Hall. In the churchyard, above the River Lowther, is the *Lowther Mausoleum* (1857). Wordsworth's association with the Lowther family is the subject of his poem, *The Earl of Lonsdale*.

In early August, the Horse Trials draw enthusiasts from all over northern England and from overseas.

Lowther Wildlife Park (open in summer) largely confines its exhibits to European species, with a special interest in deer. There are play areas for children, and plenty of room for picnics and walks. *Shap Abbey* ruin stands 4½m S.

Lyth Valley C3
Dale off A590/A5074, SW of Kendal

The dale through which the River Gilpin flows is usually called the Lyth Valley. It is a glacial valley between the limestone ridges of Whitbarrow and

Underbarrow, well known for its damson blossom in spring and its fruit in late summer. A scattering of cottages, farms and small woodlands completes the scene.

Martindale   C2
Dale SW of Penrith by A592 and minor roads

Martindale is a short dale in a crease in the fells S of Ullswater's middle reaches. The foot is at Howtown, and the dale proper is reached by a notoriously steep hill, Martindale Hause. The Victorian church, *St Peter's*, is at the top of the hill. Beyond, a narrow road descends to the original church, **St Martin's** (17th-c.), a typical dale church, stark and endearingly simple. Beyond and above is Martindale Common, over which the Martindale red deer roam.

Maryport   A2
Pop. 11,600. On W coast 6½m NW of Cockermouth on A594 (A596). EC Wed MD Fri. Inf: Tel (090081) 3738

Maryport was originally Ellenfoot, but in the boom years of the late 18th-c. local landowner Humphrey Senhouse built and extended the town and port, and named it after his wife, Mary. Coal and iron mines and shipbuilding were the industries. Later depressions bit hard, and the town is now still struggling to find a new identity, with the somewhat conflicting options of improving the harbour as a holiday facility, or offering sites for chemical industries. There is a very commendable **Maritime Museum**, which is still being improved, down by the quay.

During the Roman occupation, Maryport was a key port and supply centre, linked with coastal defences all the way to Hadrian's Wall and S into the interior. The important fort of Alauna was N of the town, covering 5¾ acres. There was an extensive civil settlement, and the many archaeological finds, including a series of altars, give a good record of the garrisons during the occupation of the site up to the 5th c.

Good views across the Solway can be enjoyed from *Mote Hill*.

Mayburgh   C2
Ancient monument to W of A6 nr Eamont Bridge on S outskirts of Penrith

This puzzling Bronze Age henge monument, hemmed in by the M6 and A6, consists of a circular bank of 'river bottom' stones built to a height of up to 15ft and enclosing some 1½ acres. There is one entrance through the rim, and a single remaining 9ft-high stone in the centre.

A short distance away, but on the E side of the A6, is '**King Arthur's Round Table**', another henge of the same period consisting of a 5ft-high circular bank around a ditch, 300ft in diameter. There are two entrances. Both these sites have been considerably disturbed, and stones removed: their original purpose remains a mystery.

1m E along the River Eamont is *Brougham* Castle.

Millom   B4
Town on SW coast on A5093, 7½m SW of Broughton-in-Furness. EC Wed. Inf (in season): Tel (0657) 2555

Millom grew rapidly from a village into a prosperous boom town after fine-quality iron ore was found in 1843, at Hodbarrow, S of the town. Vast quantities of ore were mined, and to prevent flooding from the sea, three barriers were built one after the other. A devastating depression occurred in the 1920s; other setbacks since then have been met with industrial revitalisation schemes which are still in progress.

One prospect, at present, is the development of a holiday industry. The potential is here: the town has a good, friendly shopping centre. A caravan site, on a scale which is the subject of controversy, is being built on the old mine site, while along the sandy coast to the W, around Haverigg, the excellent natural facilities for water sports are also being developed. Plans for further reclamation of the ironworks will create a large area of open parkland. The old railway house is to be converted to a permanent exhibition centre, and there is a very good **Folk Museum** which tells the story of Millom's iron industry.

Work is in progress on the castle

ruin, 1m N of the town, an imposing medieval *Pele Tower* partly occupied by a farmhouse. It has had its share of strife from the Scottish raids, the Wars of the Roses, and the Civil War. It is hoped that the castle will be open to the public before long. Just S of the castle is *Holy Trinity Old Church*, a late Norman building of red sandstone, with Victorian restorations. A wholly Victorian *Church* of the same dedication, situated in the town, recalls Millom's prosperous mining period. The decline of the iron works, and the closures which have taken place during the present century, have been described vividly by the poet Norman Nicholson, who is a native of Millom.

Milnthorpe   C4
Village on A6, 8m S of Kendal. EC Thur MD Fri

Milnthorpe was once a port bringing in coal, iron and grain; and sulphur and saltpetre for the gunpowder mills. The vital finished black powder was also one of its exports. From 1819 the Lancaster-Kendal canal took much of its trade, and in 1857 the final blow came when the port was sealed off by the building of a viaduct for the Furness railway across the estuary below. Now the once-busy port is a village serving agriculture and tourism, and the main activity is the Friday market.

A fine sight in its deer park just outside Milnthorpe is *Dallam Tower*, a grand house built in the early 18th c. The porch, with Tuscan columns, was added in the 1820s. The house is not open to the public, but at the village of *Preston Patrick*, about 4m NE of the town, the 14th-c. *Manor House* can be visited by appointment. It has a tunnel-vaulted chamber and passage, and was probably first built as a pele tower. At *Beetham* (1m S of Milnthorpe) is the Heron Corn Mill, which still grinds flour.

Muncaster Castle   A3
Historic house off A595, 1m E of Ravenglass

The seat of the Pennington family began as a 14th-c. pele tower. The tower survives as part of the present house built of local granite by Anthony

Salvin (1862). Another tower was built at the NW end to balance the design: the result is very pleasing. The rooms contain good furniture, paintings and sculpture of various dates, much of it 16th- and 17th-c. The *Gardens* alone are worth a visit. The collection of rhododendrons is without equal, and a visit in early summer can be an unforgettable experience. From the terrace there is one of the finest views in the Lake District: up the Esk Valley to the highest mountains in England. There are two *Nature Trails* in the grounds.

An 18th-c. *monument* to the NE commemorates the supposed meeting of Henry VI with an estate shepherd, after the king had fled from the defeat at Towton (1461). Tradition has it that he received sanctuary at the castle, and subsequently presented the family with a bowl since known as ' The Luck of Muncaster'.

Near Sawrey see *Sawrey*

Newby Bridge see *Windermere Lake*

Newton Arlosh   B1
Village on B5307, 3½m NE of Abbeytown

The one-time important port of Skinburness on the Solway, so useful to Holm Cultram Abbey and subsequently to Edward I on his Scottish campaigns, was swept away early in the 14th c. by catastrophic storms. The surviving population moved E to resettle in the shelter of Moricambe Bay. In 1303, the Abbot of Holme Cultram gave the people a charter to build a new church. They decided to fortify the building against Scottish raiders and, as a result, **St John's Church** has a heavy defensive pele tower, and a nave with a very narrow door – allowing only one person through at a time. On the approach of raiders, villagers would enter the tower through the door and the iron door beyond, cattle being driven into the nave.

An amusing tradition of this church is that after a marriage the first of the couple out of the church will be 'boss'.

Patterdale
C2/C3

Village on A592, 8m N of Ambleside. Event:
Patterdale Sheepdog Trials (late Summer Bank
Hol Sat)

Ringed by mountains on all sides but
the N, at Ullswater's head, Patterdale is
the obvious and best approach for the
popular Striding Edge ascent of *Helvellyn*. Since the informal car park in
the field off the Grisedale road was
closed by the landowner with the
approval of the planners, however,
there is hardly any parking facility in
the village, and car-borne walkers
must start the climb from *Glenridding*
1½m N. No hardship, but from
entirely the wrong valley.

The village owes its name to the dedication of **St Patrick's Church**. Did St
Patrick come this way, as tradition
would have it? Dedications to Celtic
saints suggest early foundations, but
the present church, by Anthony Salvin,
is largely 19th-c. The church is worth a
visit to see *tapestries* by Ann MacBeth,
a most original artist who lived in Patterdale on retirement. She died in 1948.
The tapestries depict the Nativity and
'The Good Shepherd', with the local
mountains as backgrounds. *St Patrick's
Well* is 1m N of the village, on the left
of the road along the lake shore.

On Patterdale's 'Dog's Day', sheepdog trials held since 1901 demonstrate
the working skill of fell farmers and
their dogs (Border collies).

Penrith
C2

Pop 11,600. 18m S of Carlisle (A6/M6). Event:
Penrith Show (Jul). EC Wed MD Tue, Sat. Inf:
Tel (0768) 64671 or 67126

The old red sandstone town of Penrith
has a well-settled, functional look about
it. It received its market charter 760
years ago, and is still one of the leading
markets in the county, serving farms
and rural communities over a wide area.
It has endured much over its long history. Once by agreement with the Norman barons it became part of Scotland,
but was taken back for England by
Edward I. In retaliation, when Scottish
raiders had the upper hand in the 14th
c., the town was wasted and burnt
twice; so William Strickland (later to
become Archbishop of Canterbury) was
given license to build a castle in 1397.
Building was continued to a square plan
shortly afterwards by Ralph Neville,
when he was given the town and manor.

Later the castle was occupied by a
more powerful Neville, Richard Earl of
Warwick, 'Warwick the King Maker'.
Richard of Gloucester (later Richard
III) married Anne, the earl's daughter,
and the king took residence in the 1470s
when he became the firm-handed Warden of the Western Marches, keeping
the peace on the border and enforcing
the border laws. His base was Carlisle
Castle, but his home was at Penrith, and
he fitted the castle out like a palace.
After Richard's death at Bosworth
Field the castle's fortunes declined. It
became a ruin, and the stone was taken
for building. In the notorious 'ill week'
following Elizabeth I's death in 1603,
Scottish raiders, bypassing Carlisle,
swept in and plundered an undefended
Penrith. The Graham clan was blamed,
and was cruelly punished on James I's
accession. There is still a substantial
part of the castle's S wall to be seen, and
the E and SE towers.

St Andrew's Church was not spared
by the raids, and the present handsome
building is largely Georgian. The
tower, built like a defensive refuge, is
part of the original stone structure and
possibly of the 12th c., although the
site, before then, may have been
occupied by a Saxon church. In the
churchyard to the N is the peculiar
'*Giant's Grave*' which in fact is a group
consisting of two 10th-c. crosses, with
stone hogbacks between. The nearby
'*Giant's Thumb*' is a smaller cross. To
the SW in Bishop's Yards is an old
building with a sandstone bay window,
bearing the date 1563. This may have
been *Dame Birkett's School* where William and Dorothy Wordsworth (aged 7
and 6) began their first lessons. Another
pupil was Mary Hutchinson, later to become William's wife. E of the church is
the handsome 18th-c. *Mansion House*,
now the offices of the Eden District
Council. There is another very fine
18th-c. building, *Hutton Hall*, to the
NE in Friargate.

In the market square is *The George Hotel*, where Bonnie Prince Charlie lodged during the '45 rebellion. To the W of the square is the *Cornmarket*, which has open stalls on market days. Two old houses here are now public houses. *The Gloucester Arms* is said to have been the residence of Richard Duke of Gloucester, and to date from the 15th c. Two white boars over an entrance may suggest authenticity, for a white boar was Richard's badge, but they are crudely carved. On the S side of the Cornmarket, sitting behind a yard, is *The Two Lions Inn*. This was once a residence, and dates from 1584. NW of the market square, in Middlegate, is *Robinson's School*, dated 1670, which is now used as the *Tourist Information Centre*.

Castlegate leads SW from the Cornmarket to the **Castle**, and on the way up this hill is a gem of a museum, not to be missed by the mechanically-minded. Grown from Stalker's Works, which produced anything from steam traction engine parts to manhole covers, is **Penrith Steam Museum**. Magnificent monster traction engines and rollers, a steam mill engine, a mechanical organ and many other models are on display, and there is also a working blacksmith's shop, a foundry, and a Victorian furnished cottage.

The obvious walk from the town is up to **Penrith Beacon**. This is an easy walk, and the view from the top is excellent. Ullswater can be seen, and some of the central and northern fells; E is the Pennine scene, and N is a view across the Solway into Scotland. The Beacon 'pike' was built in 1719, but for long before that the hilltop site had been used to flash warnings.

6m NW of Penrith (B5305) is the historic house, *Hutton-in-the-Forest*. S of the town, on the Cockermouth road, the *Weatheriggs Country Pottery* can be visited.

Pillar   B3
Fell SE of Ennerdale

Pillar is the fell seen impressively in the long view up Ennerdale. The bulky

summit rises to 2927ft, but the name of the fell comes from the gnarled detached rock, roughly conical in shape, on the fell's N side. For the rock climber it offers up to 500ft of climbs graded from 'easy' to 'extreme'. The first recorded ascent was by a local man, John Atkinson, in July 1826, before rock climbing was thought of as a sport; since then, many routes have been pioneered. The fell is too remote to attract many. The shortest way is from *Wasdale Head*, across *Black Sail Pass*.

Place Fell   C2
NE of Patterdale

Place Fell dominates the E view over the higher reaches of Ullswater. From *Patterdale*, its side appears as a steep and craggy wilderness. Scale is difficult to judge, but if the eye detects some movement, binoculars might pick out wandering deer on Martindale, 2m or so beyond. The summit is at 2154ft, and is most easily reached by a path from the S. The W view, of course, takes in the whole of Helvellyn's most interesting side. To the E is an exceptional view over the Pennines.

Pooley Bridge see *Ullswater*

Ravenglass   A3
Village on SW coast off A595, 6m S of Gosforth.
Inf (in season): Tel (06577) 278

Ravenglass has a typically wide Cumberland street ending at a launching ramp, for this is a little harbour at the converging estuaries of the Esk, Mite and Irt. It was probably a harbour in ancient times, and it was certainly so during the Roman Occupation. The Romans built a fort here, *Glannaventa*, 'the town on the bank'. Its stones have gone and the railway has been driven through the site, but one exciting part remains in the shape of the *bath-house* across the railway line to the S. Here the walls reach almost their original height, and they have their original pink plaster. The Roman road that crosses *Hardknott Pass* linked this fort with *Galava*, at Ambleside.

The 19th-c. **Ravenglass and Eskdale Railway** once transported iron ore and quarry stone from Boot in Eskdale. Now the 15in-gauge line carries passengers, with steam engines the normal pulling power. the 45-min journey to *Boot*, with its pretty dale church (*St Catherine's*), offers 6m of close encounters with lovely scenery, and a delightful walk from Dalegarth Station to Stanley Gill (see *Walk 8*, p.32). A little *Museum* at Ravenglass Station explains the line's history.

Just N at *Drigg Point* is Ravenglass Gullery Nature Reserve, which requires entry by permit, and further N is *Seascale*, a small seaside resort, largely Victorian, with a sandy beach.

2m NW of Ravenglass on the A595 is **Muncaster Mill**, a fully restored working water mill (open summer only) producing stone-ground flour. 1¼m E of Ravenglass, in the Esk valley, is *Muncaster Castle*, surrounded by its beautiful grounds.

Red Bank
B3(A)
Pass on minor road 1m S of Grasmere village

The road from Grasmere to Chapel Stile in Langdale crosses Red Bank. The route is narrow and steep, and was a formidable obstacle before the road was surfaced. The summit gives walkers access to the popular *Loughrigg Terrace* path, overlooking Grasmere.

Red Screes
C3
Fell W of Kirkstone Pass (A592)

Red Screes is a fell prominent above *Kirkstone Pass*. Its side is much broken with crags and boulders, and on the SE is scarred by a large quarry. The paths up from Kirkstone, which are largely made by explorers casually walking from the car park, have a reputation for causing many minor accidents. The usual routes to the 2541ft summit are by the ridge walk via *Snarker Pike* from Ambleside, or from *Scandale Pass* on the NW.

Rydal
B3(A)
Village off A591, 1¼m NW of Ambleside

Rydal is a small village of little significance but for the fact that Wordsworth lived here for the last 37 years of his life, and many notables of his time trudged up to Rydal Mount at the top of the road to visit the great man. **Rydal Mount** is open to the public and contains mementoes, family furniture and portraits. The garden is still laid out as the poet planned it.

Rydal Hall, below and opposite (not open to the public) is a 17th-c. house with a Victorian extension. This was the house of the Le Flemings, Wordsworth's landlords, who made their fortune with the Coniston copper mines. The 19th-c. *St Mary's Church* is sited below just as Wordsworth suggested, but the building did not meet with his complete satisfaction. It contains a memorial to Dr Thomas Arnold, his wife and their son, Matthew, the poet. Behind it is *Dora's Field* (NT) – a field planted with daffodils by Wordsworth for the delight of his daughter.

Rydal is the popular starting point for the ascent of *Fairfield*. The old road to *Grasmere* runs W from just above Rydal Mount, and is now an attractive public bridleway (see *Walk 2*, p.31). A wood on the right up the track above Rydal Mount has a path following *Rydal Beck* to the view of a modest but picturesque waterfall in a wooded ravine.

To the SW lies *Rydal Water*.

Rydal Water
B3(A)
Lake beside A591, 1½m NW of Ambleside

Rydal Water is a small lake with reedy banks. Its serenity, which Wordsworth enjoyed, is now marred by the A591 which runs close to its N shore. At least the view has not changed. By the roadside is *Nab Cottage*. Wordsworth's contemporary man of letters, Thomas de Quincey, lived here as a lodger, and married his landlord's daughter Peggy Simpson. Wordsworth thought he had married much beneath him, but it was a happy marriage. Later, when the De Quinceys had moved to Wordsworth's old cottage in Grasmere, Nab Cottage was occupied by Samuel Taylor Coleridge's son Hartley.

A path runs close to Rydal Water's S

bank, reached by a footbridge from the A595. It continues to *Loughrigg Terrace* above **Grasmere*, but a path branching N leads to *White Moss Common*, a popular picnic area. (See also **Grasmere* and *Walk 2*, p.31).

St Bees   A3
Village on W coast off B5345, 3½m W of Egremont

St Bega was a 7th-c. Celtic saint, whom tradition credits with the foundation of a nunnery here. There is no evidence to support this: what is certain is that a Benedictine priory was founded here in the 12th c., and that it held a great amount of property, including iron and coal mines and salt pans. It suffered greatly from Scottish raids, and the parish **Church of St Mary and St Bega** is the only part to survive the Dissolution and subsequent neglect.

There is a very fine Norman *doorway* which belonged to the original church before a rebuilding in the late 12th c. Inside, the church has features of the first building, medieval restorations and major work of the 19th c.

The village has little else of note, but there is a good beach. Nearby is *St Bees Head*, a sandstone cliff up to 322ft high, on which fulmars, razorbills, kittiwakes and guillemots nest. The path from the beach to the lighthouse on the head is only for the sure-footed.

St John's-in-the-Vale   B2
Dale on B5322, E of Keswick

St John's-in-the-Vale runs due N from the head of Thirlmere to Threlkeld, with the N spur of the Helvellyn range to the E, and Naddle Fell to the W. The view up the valley to Blencathra, particularly if there is snow on the mountain, is Alpine. At the dale's SE end is the *Castle Rock of Triermain*. Popular with rock climbers, this feature became well-known to Victorians after Sir Walter Scott's description in *The Bridal of Triermain*; an elaborate ancient castle which magically melted into a heap of rock on close approach. Imaginative early tourists would point out battlements and buttresses.

84

The delightful little Church, **St John's**, which gives the dale its name, sits high on the pass at the N end of Naddle Fell. The building is not old, but located on an old chapel site. Notable in the churchyard is the headstone of John Richardson (1817-1866), who helped his builder father rebuild the school, and was later schoolmaster there for 22 years. He was also a very gifted dialect poet.

Salkeld, Great and Little   C2
Villages 6m NE of Penrith (B6412/A686)

Located on either side of the River Eden, the two villages are quiet and handsome. At **Great Salkeld**, *St Cuthbert's Church* has a massively thick tower, built in the 14th c. to house the villagers and their possessions in the event of a Scottish raid. There is a fine Norman doorway to the nave. **Little Salkeld** has a working *Flour Mill* open to the public, selling its own produce. A path leads N from this village by the river bank to *Lacey's Caves*, mysterious chambers cut into a sandstone cliff. The megalithic circle, **Long Meg and Her Daughters*, is within easy walking distance.

Sawrey, Far and Near   C3(B)
Villages on B5285, 2½m and 2m from Bowness-on-Windermere (via ferry)

The first of the villages on the way from the ferry to Hawkshead is **Far Sawrey**, so named for being farthest from Hawkshead. ½m further on is **Near Sawrey**, a village whose name should be known to children of all ages brought up on the Beatrix Potter stories. Here is the author's cottage, **Hill Top**, owned by the National Trust. Open to the public, the cottage is however very small and will not take too many people at a time (expect to wait at busy times). The village pub, *The Tower Bank Arms*, is also owned by the NT and is just as Miss Potter painted it.

Sca Fell   B3
Fell SE of Wasdale Head

Sca Fell is chopped off from Scafell Pike by a gap, Mickledore. At 3165ft it is the lesser in height by 45ft. The route direct from one fell to the other is by a tricky little rock-climb, *Broad Stand*, a notorious trap for the unwary. The prudent fell walker takes a longer route, on the E side, by *Fox Tarn*. The easy ascent route from *Wasdale* is by *Green How*. The N face of Sca Fell is 1000ft of almost vertical crag, offering some of the longest and best rock climbs in the country. It has claimed lives, and some of the victims lie in the churchyard at Wasdale Head. The only route for fell walkers from this side of the fell is by a gully known as *Lord's Rake*, but it is not for novices, and is dangerous in winter.

Scafell Pike (NT) B3
Fell E of Wasdale Head

The routes to Scafell Pike are beaten hard. People of all kinds – male and female, young and old, professional and untried – walk boldly or struggle painfully to the 3210ft peak, for this is the highest place in England. The 'Pikes of Scafell' feature a number of peaks: NW of the highest point is *Lingmell*, and NE *Broad Crag*, *Ill Crag* and *Great End*. But only the highest will do; the rest are neglected.

Many who try to reach the summit do not make it. They under-estimate the distance and time: the shortest route, from *Wasdale Head via Lingmell and Mickledore*, can take 4½ hours for the round trip. The weather, too, can force a reversal. It is still not appreciated that while it might be spring in the dales, on the exposed Scafells conditions can still be Arctic.

The short route from Wasdale Head is the only one that can be recommended to those unfamiliar with the Lake District's rough terrain. The longer routes, such as the one from Keswick by *Sty Head* and the *Corridor Route*, are most interesting, but require some map-reading ability. It is a long step from *Langdale via Rossett Gill*, with its loose stones, and *Esk Hause*, where many go adrift in fog. The exciting route for the experienced is by the long walk up the *Upper Esk and Cam Spout*, the latter with its wild steps (the descent of which was described so fearfully and vividly by Samuel Taylor Coleridge, who did it alone in 1802). The link with *Sca Fell via Broad Stand* is not for walkers. The view from the much broken summit is, as one should expect, very extensive.

Scout Scar C3
Fell off A591 (M6), W of Kendal

Due W from Kendal's town hall, All Hallows Lane leads into a minor road climbing onto a limestone scar. At the summit there is a car park (NP) on the right. Opposite, a path leads to the top of a limestone cliff with a startling view over the green valleys of Underbarrow and Gilpin, across to the high fells of the central lakes. Not to be missed by those in the area.

Sedbergh D3
Small town on A684 (M6), 9½m E of Kendal.
Thur MD Wed. Inf (in season): Tel (0587) 20125

Sedbergh was annexed by Cumbria in the boundary changes of 1974. It is properly a Yorkshire town, and is, in fact, in the Yorkshire Dales National Park. It is a handsome stone-built settlement. *St Andrew's Church* dates from the 12th c., and there is evidence of Norman work in its much altered structure. The town has a number of 18th and 19th-c. buildings associated with Sedbergh School. To the SW is *Brigflatts Quaker Meeting House* (17th-c.). This simple whitewashed house has associations with George Fox and the early Quakers.

Shap C2
Village on A6 (M6), 9m S of Penrith. EC Thur, Sat MD Mon

Shap village is on the high moor which travellers S to N must cross. It was a staging post on this much travelled road from pre-Roman times, and stands some 800ft above sea level. Local industry is quarrying: there is exceptionally fine granite in the fell. There are signs of Neolithic settlement in the area, notably the **standing stones** to the W of the village. *St Michael's Church* dates from the 12th c. In the main street is the *Market House* of the 17th c.

1¼m to the W by minor roads is **Shap Abbey**, founded by Premonstratensians (White Canons) in the late 12th c. Much of the stone has been removed, but the early 16th-c. W tower remains. The ruins in their river valley are cared for by the DoE.

Silecroft
A4
Village on A5093, 3m NW of Millom

There is nothing of note in Silecroft, but it has the best sandy bathing beach in the district, fronted by a pebbly strand seemingly representing most of the Lake District's geology. There is a clear-day view of the Isle of Man. From nearby Whicham there is a good starting point for the ascent of *Black Combe (1970ft).

Silloth
A1
Village on NW coast (B5302/B5300), 13m N of Maryport. EC Tue. Inf (in season): Tel (0965) 31944

Although there were high hopes for Silloth's development as a resort when the village was laid out in the mid-19th c., it never really succeeded, perhaps because of its distance from the rail network. It is, however, a very attractive place, with its seaside terraces separated from the sea front by a pleasant green planted with fir trees. The small commercial harbour does not detract, and there are fine views of the Galloway Hills, especially at sunset. There are a number of camping and caravanning sites in the area, a beach and a golf course.

Sizergh Castle (NT)
C3
Historic house off A6 (M6/A591), 3m S of Kendal

Sizergh Castle has been the seat of the Strickland family since the 13th c. Like other great houses in the area, it consists of a Hall built onto a pele tower. The tower here dates from the 14th c., and is exceptionally massive. The Hall was added, and then extended, in the 15th and 18th c. Sizergh is famed for its great wealth of Elizabethan wood carving, including five elaborate *chimney pieces*. The top floor of the old tower serves as a museum.

The *Garden*, with its rock garden and waterfalls, and collection of rare ferns, is beautifully kept. House and garden are in the care of the NT.

*Levens Hall and its topiary gardens are 3m to the S.

Skelwith Force (NT)
B3(A)
Waterfall at Skelwith Bridge off A593, 2½m W of Ambleside

These dramatic falls on the River Brathay, close to Skelwith Bridge, can also be reached by an attractive walk from the village at *Elter Water (see *Walk 3*, p.31).

Skiddaw
B2
Fell N of Keswick

Skiddaw sprawls over 14 sq m and is prominent in the N view from many localities. The peak stands at 3053ft. The mountain is scorned by many enthusiastic fell walkers, as its terrain is of less interest than those in the Volcanic Series, further S. The contours are rounded and there are few crags, for the rock is Skiddaw Slate, a friable material. It is, though, a splendid fell with spectacular viewpoints, and it has the merit of being the ideal first fell walk for the uninitiated – though a serious slog. The usual ascent route from *Keswick is by the side of *Latrigg* to the NE of the town, and by the very clear path all the way NW. The summit is an airy plateau. Subsidiary peaks also offering fine prospects are *Ullock Pike* to the W and *Carl Side* to the SW; and *Little Man* to the SE, which gives the best views over Derwent Water and to the central fells.

Steeple
B3
Fell SE of Ennerdale

Steeple's name is obviously suggested by its shape, as seen from Ennerdale. It is in an area of crags noted for drama (*Pillar is little more than 1m away to the NE). However, its peak (2687ft) is easily reached by the experienced walker without any rock climbing, either direct from *Ennerdale or from *Wasdale by the ridge route through *Red Pike*, or by *Scoat Tarn*.

Sty Head
B3
Mountain pass on bridle path, 2m NE of Wasdale Head

'Stand at Sty Head long enough, and every mountaineer in the world will pass you by'. So it was once said. But that was in the days when most mountaineers were British, and the wide world was not so accessible. The Sty is still nonetheless a major fell crossroads between Borrowdale and Wasdale, crossing the fell at 1600ft. One path goes S by the *Corridor Route* to *Scafell Pike*, and another W to *Great Gable*. *Styhead Tarn* softens the craggy landscape, and here is a popular mountaineer's camp site.

Swinside Stone Circle
B3
Ancient monument off A595, 4½m W of Broughton-in-Furness

The stone circle at Castlerigg, Keswick is well known. If Swinside were more accessible, the circle here would be, too. The choice of site under the NE end of Black Combe has no apparent explanation, but this is one of many Bronze-Age sites found in the SW area of the Lake District. The stones (there are more than 50) are more closely placed than Castlerigg's, and set in an almost perfect circle. Although it can be viewed from a public path, the circle is on farm land and permission must be obtained for a closer approach.

Tarn Hows (NT)
B3(A)
Beauty spot off B5285, 3m NW of Hawkshead

The best known beauty spot in the S of the Lake District has a subtle chemistry that is instantly captivating. Viewed from the S, the tarn lies placidly below, screened by a mixture of broadleaves and conifers, with the contrasting drama of a fell view – the Langdale Pikes – beyond. The scene is partly man-made; early this century three large pools were made one, and the surrounding trees planted.

The area is at its colourful best in autumn and spring, but at peak holiday times car parking can be impossible. There is a pleasant walk round the tarn (see *Walk 9*, p.32).

Taylor Gill Force
B3
Waterfall in Borrowdale, 1m S of Seathwaite

Taylor Gill Force falls for 100ft down a wild and craggy ravine by a scramblers' path to *Sty Head* along the W bank of *Styhead Gill*. For the sure-footed – and those who do not suffer from vertigo – the sight is worth pursuing.

Temple Sowerby
D2
Village on A66, 6½m E of Penrith

A neat little village grouped around a green, close to the River Eden. The name comes from the ancient owners of Sowerby Manor, the Knights Templar. **Acorn Bank** (NT) to the N is a garden open to the public. It has a walled rose garden and a comprehensive collection of herbs, as well as herbaceous plants and spring flowers.

Thirlmere
B2
Lake beside A591, 6½m SE of Keswick

Thirlmere is about 4m long, and is well seen from the A591. It was once Leathes Water, and its village of Wythburn was strangely called 'the City'. Wythburn, and the settlement to the NE at Armboth, were drowned in 1894 when the dam was built and the water level raised 50ft for a Manchester Corporation reservoir. Only the little *Church* of Wythburn remains, to the E of the A591. The catchment area is extensively planted with conifers, giving it an alien, Scandinavian atmosphere. The fluctuating lake level produces a white rim which detracts from a natural appearance. Even so it has its admirers, and since the Water Authority has removed its access prohibitions to the lake's shore line it has become popular.

The lake holds trout, perch and pike: the forest a herd of red deer. On either side of the lake, a nature trail can be followed through the woods (*Launchy Ghyll* W, *Swirls Forest* E).

Tilberthwaite Gill
B3(A)
Waterfall off A593, 2½m N of Coniston

Like many of the district's waterfalls, the volume of water dropping down to Tilberthwaite from Wetherlam responds rapidly to rainstorms, but the flow is as quickly diminished. After heavy rain, Tilberthwaite Gill (NP) is worth a visit. In Victorian times it was possible to walk up the gill by a series of bridges. In time these have been swept away. The path now crosses the gill from the S bank, and there is a viewpoint bridge just below the main fall. Further exploration can be hazardous and is not recommended.

Troutbeck C3(A)
Village off A592, 3m N of Windermere

Troutbeck's church is isolated from its village, standing by the beck and the A592. The village is above it, stretching along a parallel minor road. This follows the W flank of the long wild valley of the Trout Beck which flows S into Windermere.

The village is a collection of 17th and 18th-c. buildings grouped around communal wells, each dedicated to a saint. At the S end is **Townend** (NT), a typical 17th-c. yeoman's house containing oak furnishings worked by local hands. It is open to the public, and gives an illuminating picture of local 17th-c. life. One of the village inns, *The Mortal Man*, was famous for selling Sally Birkett's ale, which was notoriously strong. The church (*Jesus Chapel*) has stained glass windows by William Morris and Sir Edward Burne-Jones.

To the N, on the E side of the A592, is *Troutbeck Park* (NT): there is an airy view of it on the descent from Kirkstone Pass. The Tongue was once occupied by an ancient British settlement: the pretty farm now here was once managed by Beatrix Potter.

Ullswater C2
Lake 5m SW of Penrith. Inf (in season): Pooley Bridge Tel (08536) 530; Glenridding Tel (08532) 414

Ullswater is the region's second largest lake, a little less than 8m long, and with two distinct bends to it. Some reckon the lake superior in beauty to Windermere, but there are distinct differences. Unlike Windermere, Ullswater has its head in the steep Borrowdale Volcanic rocks, and its feeders pour off Helvellyn

to the SW and off a tangle of rough fells to the SE. From the middle reaches the landscape changes rapidly, as the lake penetrates the more friable Skiddaw Slates, and at the foot there are flatter plains of limestone and sandstone stretching towards Penrith.

The Ullswater Navigation Company runs a 'steamer' service in the season. The journey S, from *Pooley Bridge* pier, offers the best view of the changing scene. Behind the pier is **Dunmallot**, atop of which is the ruin of a ditch-and-mound Romano-British fort. The ancient British road, High Street, high to the SE, was improved by the Romans. The next pier S is at *Howtown*; no town this, but a few houses. The route then goes through the narrows with *Skelly Neb* to the N. In old times a net was spread across the lake here, to catch the 'schelly', a whitefish found only in this lake. Above to the S is *Hallin Fell*, which can be climbed easily from the minor road on its S side. Its views are among the best anywhere. *Gowbarrow Park* on the N side was once a deer park, and here Wordsworth saw his daffodils; to the W is **Aira Force** (NT) a spectacular waterfall on Aira Beck with viewing bridges in a wooded ravine. The lake then turns S, with the Helvellyn range seen to the SW and Place Fell closing in on the E. The S pier is at *Glenridding*.

The lake holds trout and perch as well as the schelly. Powered boats are allowed on the lake, but there is a 10mph speed limit on its entire length. Craft can be launched at Glenridding, and at Howtown. Light craft can be manhandled into the lake also at Glencoyne Bay. One of the best walks in the Lake District is along terraced paths on the wooded E shore (see *Walk 11*, p.32). The steamer is taken to Howtown, and clear paths are taken W and S from the pier.

Ulverston B4
Pop 12,000. On Furness peninsula 9m NE of Barrow-in-Furness (A590). EC Wed. MD Thur. Sat. Inf: Tel (0229) 52299

When Ulverston's canal was built by John Rennie (1796), linking the town to the sea and making it a port, its importance as a market town grew to the detriment of others such as Broughton and Hawkshead. At the port's peak it was clearing 600 vessels a year; the town's population grew to 50,000. The coming of the coastal railway line in 1856 killed the port, and many of its industries were attracted to rapidly growing Barrow-in-Furness, but the market remained to serve a large part of the Furness peninsula. The town is not large enough to have had its centre torn out for redevelopment, so it retains its old, friendly character, and its Thursday market is a lively and popular affair.

One of Ulverston's famous men was Sir John Barrow (1764-1848), founder of the Royal Geographical Society, who after years at sea became Under-Secretary to the Admiralty for 40 years. His books were extremely popular, and include *The Life of Lord Howe*, and *Voyages of Discovery and Research into the Arctic Regions*. Another local celebrity was Stan Laurel; the **Laurel and Hardy Museum** in Upper Brook Street has some of Stan's possessions and props, and shows a selection of Laurel and Hardy films.

Nearby *Swarthmoor* has the distinction of being the point where Lambert Simnel, with 2000 mercenaries, landed and camped in 1487 to claim the throne from Henry VII. But it has another distinction, for at **Swarthmoor Hall** lived George Fox, founder of the Society of Friends (Quakers). He married Margaret, widow of Judge Fell, in 1669, and her home at Swarthmoor became his home when he was not on his travels or in prison for his pacifist preaching. His wife, whom he had converted, and who was equally ardent in her belief, shared his privations. The Hall, and Elizabethan house, is in the ownership of the Society of Friends, and is open to the public.

On *The Hoad*, a hill to the NW of the town, stands a scaled-down replica of the Eddystone Light as a memorial to Sir John Barrow. The ascent of the hill makes a popular walk.

Urswick B4
Village on Furness peninsula off A590, 3m S of Ulverston. Event: Rush-bearing procession (Sun nearest to St Michael's Day, Sep 29)

The houses of Great and Little Urswick are ranged around a small tarn which inevitably has its legend of a 'sunken village'. To the W are **Urswick Stone Walls**, the remains of an Iron-Age settlement. The **Church of St Mary and St Michael** is oddly placed, away from the villages. This often suggests an ancient establishment on an earlier, pagan site. The church, with its imposing tower, is not an old building but worth a visit for its superb woodcarving, the work of the Chipping Campden Guild (1909-12). When the earthen church floor was strewn with rushes in old times a fresh supply was brought in regularly. The practice continues as an annual ceremony today, when the village children process with flowers and rushes from the tarn, through each village in turn and then to the church.

Wasdale B3
Dale E of Gosforth

Wasdale is the dale running SW from under Sca Fell. Its SE wall, the well-known *Wast Water* Screes, is an unstable 3m-long, 1700ft cliff which occasionally tumbles rock into Wast Water as it has done since the last Ice Age. The hamlet of *Nether Wasdale (Strands)* is at the dale's foot. To the E of it a footpath goes from Woodhow down into *Low Wood* (NT) and here, along the shoreline path passing *Wasdale Hall* (now a youth hostel), are the best lake views. The lakeside road leads to the junction with the Gosforth road, below Middle Fell, which has the classic view of the Screes. Some find it disturbing, some exciting, some just beautiful; but it certainly demands a response. A *Nature Trail* can be followed from near the hamlet along the shore.

Further up-dale, *Nether Beck* flows into the lake. A path here to the left takes one by handsome falls and rock pools. Beyond is the steep end of *Yewbarrow*, and from this point one sees the great hump of Sca Fell, and the Lingmell spur to Scafell Pike. The approach to Wasdale Head brings Kirk Fell into full view, and behind it looms the massive hulk of Great Gable.

Wasdale Head with its many stone walls has an inn and a shop. Behind the inn is a lovely old arched bridge, and a path N from here takes one past more waterfalls. The tiny dale **Church** is a gem, with roof timbers said to have been salvaged from a shipwreck; in the churchyard are the graves of climbers who have died on Sca Fell crag. Wasdale Head is the base for many fell walks: E up *Mosedale*, the way to *Ennerdale*, and to *Buttermere by Black Sail Pass*; NE to *Great Gable* and *Sty Head*; E by *Lingmell* to *Scafell Pike*: S to *Burnmoor and *Eskdale*. A very rough path runs along the E shore under the Screes.

Wast Water (NT)   B3
Lake 6m E of Gosforth

Wast Water is the deepest lake in England. A motor road and a footpath follow the NW shore as far as Wasdale Head; travelling NE from the foot of the lake, the full grandeur of the Lake District's high fells unfolds. **Wast Water Screes** slide into the water from the SE side to a depth of 260ft, and are best seen from the NW shoreline below Middle Fell: '. . . wrinkled and torrent-torn and barely-patched with moss. . .' noted Samuel Taylor Coleridge, on a lone expedition one August.

The lake, 3m long, is so pure that it supports little plant and animal growth, although there are trout and char. An attempt to extract water from the lake for the nuclear power industry was defeated by the National Park Authority and conservationists in 1982.

Watendlath (NT)   B2
Small village off B5289, 5m S of Keswick

Watendlath is reached by a minor road turning off the Borrowdale road 2m S of Keswick. The narrow road is rather harrowing for motorists, but there are two classic viewpoints *en route*. The first is **Ashness Bridge** (small car park) with a splendid and much photographed view of Derwent Water below and the

fells beyond (see *Walk* 7, p.32). The next is further on, up in the wood where the road runs close to a tree-clad precipice. This is '**Surprise View**' with an unexpected glimpse of Derwent Water far below (see also *Walk* 7). Watendlath is known to readers of Hugh Walpole as the home of Judith Paris. *Watendlath Tarn* is by the village, completing a pretty scene.

Whinlatter Pass   B2
Pass on B5292 (A66), 5m W of Keswick. Visitor Centre (in season): Tel (059682) 469

The Whinlatter Pass road is the easiest route from Keswick to Lorton, Loweswater and Buttermere. It passes through Thornthwaite Forest. Here the Forestry Commission have opened a **Visitor Centre** with displays and audio-visual presentations, explaining the forestry industry in this area. There are a number of walks from the centre and a *Nature Trail*. The summit of the pass is at 1040ft, but there are few steep sections.

Whitbarrow   C3
Fell off A5074 (A590), NE of Grange-over-Sands

Whitbarrow is a limestone ridge to the E of the Winster Valley. A number of public paths serve it. The highest point is only 706ft, but the views are good, and there is a sense of quiet remoteness. Part of the summit is a nature reserve in care of the Cumbria Trust for Nature Conservation.

Whitehaven   A2
Pop 27,000. On W coast 13m SW of Cockermouth (A595). EC Wed MD Thur, Sat. Inf: Tel (0946) 5678

Whitehaven is a manufacturing and mining town and harbour. It was developed in the 1680s as a coal port by the Lowther family, and is an eminent example of 17th-c. English town planning, with its streets arranged in a grid layout with one block left free for the main church, the 19th-c. *St Nicholas*.

The port of Whitehaven was once second only to London, handling twice the tonnage of Liverpool and Bristol. It declined as Liverpool grew in the 19th c., and its coal industry has since declined as workings have become un-economic.

St James Church is a Georgian master-piece, and there are other good 18th and 19th-c. buildings in the town, notably around Lowther Street and Duke Street, and along Roper Street which leads W to the quays and lighthouse of the 17th and 18th c.

The region's history and geology are illustrated in the **Whitehaven Museum** in the market place. Boats can be launched at a slipway in the S harbour by permission of the Harbour Master.

Wigton
B1

Small town on A596, 11m SW of Carlisle. Event: Wigton Horse Sales (last Wed in Oct). EC Wed MD Tue

A market charter was granted to Wig-ton in 1262. It is still a busy little town, serving a wide area on market days. It is a town worthy of exploration as there are some handsome buildings, mainly dating from the prosperous period of the 19th c. when wool and woollen goods were the town's trade. There are two prosperous-looking churches: the classical *St Mary's* (1788) and the Roman Catholic *St Cuthbert's* built in 1837 in the Gothic style. The *fountain* in the Market Place has fine marble deco-ration. The horse sales were once three-day affairs, but all is now packed into a single hectic day.

1½m SE is the Roman fort site at *Old Carlisle*. This was Olenacum, a large cavalry fort strategically placed at a Roman crossroads. Only the platform is left.

Windermere (Lake)
C3(A/B)

7m W of Kendal (A590/A591/A592). Events: Lake Festival (2nd week in Jul); Marathon (last Sun in Oct). Inf: Tel (09662) 2244. Boat registration: Tel (0539) 24555

Some Lake District visitors know only of Windermere, and further they will not go. The lake's popularity came from its ease of access; from its great size, which offers scope for varied water rec-reation; and from its acknowledged beauty. Windermere is England's largest lake: 11m long but nowhere wider than 1m, covering 3647 acres. The whole of the lake lies in the softer

Silurian series of rock, which explains the rich tree and shrub growth along its banks. From the N basin, however, there are superb views into the Borrow-dale Volcanics of the Fairfield and Langdale Fells, with the Pikes promi-nent.

There are two basins in the lake, separated by a central shallower area with islands. The N basin is the deepest, reaching 220ft. Windermere was long used as a highway before the roads were built, and remains so. It is patrolled by police and traffic wardens, and has speed limit zones like any dry highway. A summer 'steamer' service runs the length of the lake from *Lakeside* in the SW to the piers at Bow-ness and Waterhead, Ambleside.

The journey up-lake offers a wealth of varied interest and beauty. At the S end opposite the Lakeside pier is *Fell Foot Country Park* (NT), a very popular picnic area and holiday centre. Travel-ling up-lake the YMCA Youth Centre is on the W, and N of it a public footpath skirts the shore for much of the way to the ferry. On the E bank is *The Beech Hill Hotel*, and by it is a public picnic area (NP). At Storrs Hall at the end of a jetty is the 1804 eccentricity '*The Tem-ple*' (NT). N of this the lake is crossed from Bowness to the Hawkshead road by the wire-drawn ferry. Nearby is *Ferry House*, the headquarters of the Freshwater Biological Association.

Several islands lie in the shallower central area. The largest is *Belle Isle*, about ½m long, and to the W of it are the islands of *Thompson's Holme*, and the two '*Lilies of the Valley*' (NP). Just to the N of the ferry on the Bowness side is the Lake Warden's and the Police base, and a public launching ramp. *Bowness Bay* is busy with boat hire, and here is the headquarters of the Royal Windermere Yacht Club.

On the W side beyond the islands, along the wooded *Claife* shore (NT), a minor road and rough track offer public access for about 3m (see *Walk 10*, p.32). There is also a short *Nature Trail* here, starting near the ferry. N of Bowness Bay is the **Windermere Steamboat**

Museum, then **Adelaide Hill** (NT), one of the best viewpoints for the lake. After reaching the widest point, White Cross Bay is to the E, then *Wray Castle* (NT), a Victorian sham castle, can be seen to the W. Ahead on the right is *Brockhole*, the National Park Visitor Centre. The lake then spreads out with bays, the deepest *Pull Wyke* to the W. On the E shore opposite is *The Low Wood Hotel*, with a nearby water-skiing centre. The pier and boat-hire complex at *Waterhead* is then reached, where there is also a launching area for light craft. Mechanically powered boats have to be registered before launching.

Trout, pike and perch are found in the lake, but the greatest interest is in the char. This is a deepwater trout – a relic of the Ice Age. Windermere potted char were a favourite delicacy on the tables of the aristocracy in the last century. The quiet lake in winter attracts many visiting ducks and geese, including barnacle geese, greylags, goldeneyes, shelduck and red-breasted mergansers.

Newby Bridge, at the lake foot, is a hamlet with an attractive stone bridge spanning the River Leven and an old coaching house, *The Swan Inn*. Running along the riverside opposite is the **Lakeside and Haverthwaite Railway**, a 3½m branch line of the old Lancaster-Barrow-in-Furness Railway which has been revived by enthusiasts to serve the 'steamer' departure point at Lakeside.

5m NW of Newby Bridge is **Rusland Hall**, a Georgian mansion. The original part of this house, built *c.* 1720, is the three-storey central block. The rest of the house was added by the Archibald family, *c.* 1845. The greatest interest of the house lies in its mechanical music and early photographic equipment collections. There are garden walks and fine views; just S of the house along the river is the *Hay Bridge Nature Reserve* (open by appointment).

4m N of Newby Bridge on the W side of Lake Windermere is **Graythwaite Hall**, with a 7-acre landscaped garden planted with rhododendrons, azaleas and many other shrubs.

Windermere　　　　　　　　C3(A)
Town 8m NW of Kendal on A591. EC Thur (winter). Inf: Tel (09662) 4561

When the mainline railway from London to Carlisle was constructed, a branch line was planned from Oxenholme through Kendal to Low Wood, Ambleside, and possibly later by tunnel to Keswick. Its projected westernmost section, through superior landscape, received strong opposition from some landowners, and from conservationists. Wordsworth sounded the alarm in 1844, in a sonnet sent to the *Morning Post* with the oft-quoted line:

'Is then no nook of English ground secure from rash assault?'

The 'rash assault' got as far as the hamlet of Birthwaite, situated 1m NE of the old lakeside village of Bowness-on-Windermere and well above the lake, 5m short of Ambleside. In spite of the promotion of further plans, beyond this it dared not go.

Who had ever heard of Birthwaite? To indicate to travellers that the station was the nearest they could get to the lake, the railway company named it 'Windermere', and the town was born with it. Birthwaite and the surrounding villages were absorbed into a building programme of houses for new middle-class inhabitants, and of hotels and guest houses to serve the swelling tourist industry that the railway brought. The town's boundary eventually merged with that of Bowness, and it remains the Lake District's most popular tourist centre. As a 'nearly new' town there is little to see of architectural interest, though the local stone and slate has been used extensively and pleasantly and there is no jarring incongruity. A popular route on the A591 from Kendal approaches Windermere in a steep climb to the station, giving a 'surprise' view: a fine first impression for visitors.

Orrest Head, ½m N of the town, reached by an easy footpath starting across the road from the station, is arguably one of the best viewpoints in the Lake District. It takes in most of the central fells and a large stretch of the lake. **Adelaide Hill** (NT), a grassy hill by the lakeside ½m W of the town, is another very pleasant place to sit and take in the view.

Off the A592, 1m N of the town, is **Holehird Gardens**. In the grounds of a country house (not open) these attractive gardens are maintained by the Lakeland Horticultural Society and have a wide range of shrubs, alpines, heathers and flowering trees.

S of the town is the lake's boating centre at *Bowness-on-Windermere*.

Winster Valley   C3/C4
Dale off A5074, SE of Bowness-on-Windermere

The Winster Valley is not a haven for motorists, but it is a quiet area with captivating corners. Winster village has a handsome little post office, and the Winster River is followed S from the village by a road opposite *The Brown Horse*. One of the dale's gems is the little 17th-c. *St Anthony's Church* which lies beyond the hamlet of Bowland Bridge in a sanctuary-like setting. A steep road runs SW from the valley past *Gummer's How*, an easily climbed viewpoint for the foot of Windermere.

Workington   A2
Pop 29,000. On W coast 8½m W of Cockermouth (A66/A595/A596). EC Thur MD Wed, Sat

The only deep-water port between Mersey and Clyde, Workington is also a manufacturing and market town. Like its neighbour Whitehaven, the town made its fortune from coal mining and shipping; also from steel. All have declined.

Workington's better buildings reflect the prosperity of the 19th c., but there is a pleasant 18th-c. environment around *Portland Square*, with its trees and cobblestones and surrounding streets laid out in a grid plan (1775). *St John's Church* in Washington Street, an imposing copy of Inigo Jones's St Paul's in Covent Garden, was built early in the 19th c. and the tower added in 1846.

The **Helena Thompson Museum** in Park End Road is an 18th-c. house with collections representing social and local history.

Wray Castle (NT)   B3(A)
Historic house off B5286, 3¾m S of Ambleside

Never actually a castle, this Victorian pastiche is nonetheless an attractive sight. The 'castle', complete with mock ruins (most of which have been removed), was built for a Liverpool surgeon in the 1840s – as a surprise for his wife, it is said. It is also said that she did not like it. The castle is let to a school and is not open to the public, but the grounds are pleasant and include a piece of lake shore which is one of Windermere's safest bathing places. The surgeon also built a church nearby, and here for a time Canon Rawnsley, one of the founders of the National Trust, served before moving to Crosthwaite, Keswick.

Wreay   C1
Village off A6 (M6), 5m SE of Carlisle

The attraction at Wreay is a very remarkable church, built in the 1840s as a memorial to Katherine Losh by her sister Sara. Sara was talented and well travelled, and the design of *St Mary's Church* was based on much that she had admired in European architecture. The church is covered with carvings of plants, fruits, flowers and insects, and the gargoyles are reptiles. The *Mausoleum* for Katherine is built of seemingly casually placed rough rocks.

Wrynose Pass   B3
Pass 8m W of Ambleside

Second in ferocity only to *Hardknott Pass* to the W, by which its very narrow road is connected, Wrynose Pass ascends steeply to 1200ft. At its summit stands the *Three Shires Stone*, which until Local Government reorganisation in 1974 marked the converging county boundary lines. Lancashire was to the S; Cumberland to the NW; and Westmorland to the N and NE. The Roman Road can be traced with difficulty; it is generally on the N side of the modern road. It climbed from Eskdale (W) over Hardknott to Wrynose and thence through Little Langdale to link *Glannaventa* (Ravenglass) with *Galava* at Borrans Field (Ambleside).

Index

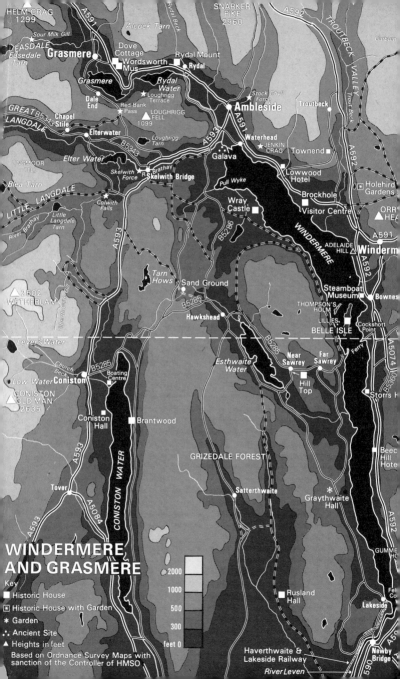

WINDERMERE
AND GRASMERE

Key
- ■ Historic House
- ⊡ Historic House with Garden
- ✳ Garden
- ∴ Ancient Site
- ▲ Heights in feet

Based on Ordnance Survey Maps with
sanction of the Controller of HMSO